ONBOARDED

Cover and book design by Tom Howey

For more information, address:
brad.giles@evolutionpartners.com.au

www.evolutionpartners.com.au

ONBOARDED

*How to bring new hires to the point
where they are effective, faster*

BRAD GILES

Brad Giles makes a compelling case for onboarding as the seed to growing incredible work place cultures and happy, contributing team members.

BEV ATTFIELD

Partner at Within People

Vancouver, Canada

At last, a book that offers executives and hiring managers the toolkit to embed their new hire into the tribe of their company in an intelligent and well thought through manner. As an executive search consultant, I cannot recommend this book and its teachings highly enough. Follow it, or risk losing the heart and mind of your new hire!

BRIAN BRISCOE

Managing Director, Briscoe Consulting

Perth, Australia

Onboarded is an essential read, full of great tips to ensure your valuable new recruits are given the structure and support needed to become highly effective team members

TIM CLARKSON

CEO, Chas Clarkson

Sydney, Australia

Onboarding well is absolutely critical to staff retention and getting the best results from your team. Brad's book nails it, explaining why it's important and how to do it. A must read for all managers.

DAMIAN COLLINS

Chairman, Westbridge Funds Management

Managing Director, Momentum Wealth

Perth, Australia

Brad brings a level of rigor, experienced insight and practical tools to a key challenge in the market of growth companies: a clear definition and solution to onboarding in organizations. What makes Brad's content and tools so valuable is that they are forged from personal experience as a business leader, successful work as a coach to business leaders, and the research of listening to his coaching peers and leaders worldwide. After reading this book, please get it into the hands of others so we can solve this key challenge as a community of readers worldwide.

KEITH CUPP
Gravitas Impact Premium Coaching
Portland, Oregon

Onboarded takes something that can feel like a rarefied luxury -- a great onboarding experience that might only be the privilege of huge enterprises, or boutique startups -- and presents it to the reader as an accessible practice in the truest sense: an understandable collection of processes, actions and behaviours that can be learned, measured, and optimized by anyone, anywhere. Even better, the reader is encouraged in the belief that these practices can be mastered. They can, and by you.

JOSH GARDNER
Director of Information Technology, General Fusion
Vancouver, Canada

Onboarding is the great unspoken problem that probably haunts many businesses but especially scale ups. Reading this book helped us with this recurrent issue in a very positive way. It's thoroughly researched and very level headed, reminiscent in some ways of another definitive management book, Good to Great. If you're running a growing business this book is a must.

DR. JEMMA GREEN
Cofounder & Chairman, Powerledger
Perth, Australia

Onboarding has been a significant blockage to not only our business but also the entire real estate industry. Brad Giles through the use of Technique & Technology has delivered us a permanent solution that now enables us to truly scale.

PHIL HARRIS
Managing Director Harris Real Estate
Adelaide, Australia

In an era where competition for skilled staff has never been fiercer and the expectations of staff on companies has never been higher, onboarding and retention strategies are more important now than ever. By implementing Brad Giles onboarding strategies outlined in this book our team retention for new starters within the first 12 months doubled which had a huge impact on the culture of Aventus and ultimately our financial results. This book is a must read for any leader or manager looking to create a high performance and winning culture.

DARREN HOLLAND
CEO Aventus
Sydney

Finally a book that pays attention to, in my opinion, the most important influence on a business' culture – a manual on making sure you have the right people boarding the bus, that they know where to sit, fully aware of the destination and what it'll take to get there. Well done Brad, another glaring hole in the business growth and leadership reading list covered!

SAM HYDER
CEO, Geographe Enterprises
Perth, Australia

Onboarded is the secret weapon of great teams. We previously whipped through our onboarding process, without any idea of how fiercely important it is, the enormous impact it has on culture and the cost of getting it wrong. Never again!

CATH JULES
Founder, The Hatchery
Sydney, Australia

Effective onboarding new team members is the starting point of building a great organization. Yet most companies do a terrible job of it. Brad outlines the cultural and financial costs then delivers a thorough approach for getting it right and a plan for how to implement it in your organization. Your winning team starts here.

DR KAIHAN KRIPPENDORFF

Founder, Outthinker and author of *Outthink the Competition*, *Hide a Dagger Behind a Smile* and *Way of Innovation*

New York, New York

Onboarded is the book that every leader who wants a team of A players should read and implement today.

KEVIN LAWRENCE

Chief Advisor, Lawrence & Co. Growth Advisors

Author of *Your Oxygen Mask First* & Key Contributor to *Scaling Up*

Vancouver, Canada

Onboarding is one of the biggest challenges leaders face as they run a growing organization. Many times we confuse productivity and busyness. The goal is productive. Brad details the roadmap to go from hire to productive in a simple and easy to understand way. He not only justifies the investment in good onboarding but helps readers see the real cost of poor onboarding. This book is a must read for any manager who hires people for their team. Many HR professionals can gain a powerful process for their organization and this is not taught anywhere in business education. Brad's process will improve the likelihood of success for new hires and have a positive impact on the team and company.
Brad has nailed it again.

MICHAEL MIRAU

CEO and Founder of Tribute Printing

Dallas, Texas

I instantly bought 100 copies to give to every manager I know. As a fast-growing company, the practical steps Brad provides in Onboarded have been a game-changer. Given more than 80% of our spend is on people, we can't afford unproductive new hires. Onboarded has given both us and the new starter ultra-clarity on what success is - which has been very motivating for them to work towards. We love the simple blueprint to work out if someone is a successful fit within 90 days, which has been critical to expand our high-performing team!

MICHAEL MOMSEN
Founder & CEO, Zipline.io
Australia

Brad Giles has made impossible for every leader to ignore the huge pile of elephant poop in the living room – the fact that almost all companies do a rotten job of onboarding new employees, and consequently new employees are more likely to underperform and quit. Brad outlines the extent of the problem, identifies what to do (and how and when), and in Chapter 6 presents a compelling calendar, a roadmap for any leader to follow. Additionally, he offers "helpful hints," such as assign an onboarding "buddy," responsible for tracking and implementing steps that many others should perform.

DR. BRAD SMART
CEO Topgrading Inc and author *Topgrading*

After many years working with businesses and leaders, the most significant issue is people. As this book indicates, the dynamic changes every time you bring a new team member on board. This is handled badly in most situations. This book gives very practical, well researched, and relevant guidance on the process of onboarding new staff. It flows into the importance of developing culture. Brad writes with an easy-to-read style that allows the reader to take away clear methods to bring new staff into the team, and develop a strong culture that promotes a greater output. This book has a wonderful balance between research, experience, and clear examples, leading to understanding a logical approach for dealing with staff. I recommend this book to anyone who employs staff, and is looking to build a long-term, effective team.

STEVE STANLEY

Director, WA, CEO Institute

Perth, Western Australia

This book could not have been better timed. This is a must read for all leaders right now! Great teams is how you win the game!

SHANNON SUSKO

Founder and CEO, Metronomics

Author of *Metronome Effect, 3HAG WAY* and *Metronomics*

Whistler, Canada

Entrepreneurs, CEO's and senior leaders: read this book and take action – it's practical and helpful. After 11 years ranked as one of Australia's 50 Best Places to Work, I thought our onboarding program at The Physio Co was strong. After reading Onboarded, we now have a list of things to do that will make it MUCH stronger. Thanks, Brad, for doing the heavy lifting on this super-important topic.

TRISTAN WHITE

Founder and CEO, The Physio Co

Author, *Culture Is Everything*

Melbourne, Australia

To my wife Maggie, and my children Mitchell, Reece, Cameron, and Amelie.
Thank you.

Contents

Introduction

"It's not getting any better," said Nick as he sunk into the kitchen chair. "I can't find anything. And the way they do things doesn't make sense."

Emma, his wife, sighed.

"Alex seems okay, but he's supposed to be my manager, and I've only spoken to him once in the three days since I've started." Nick groaned, then got up and stared out the window.

"Maybe you should have taken the other job in Newtown. The salary was almost the same." Emma replied.

Emma's comment didn't help Nick, and he snapped back at her.

"Have a play around with the software, they said. I don't even know what I'm supposed to be working on. It's so..." He paused, took a deep breath, and looked back out the window as if he was trying to find the words. "It's so different from the interview. It's like once you have signed the contract and get hired, they just don't care anymore."

Emma didn't want to get snapped at again, so she took a long pause before saying, "So what should you do?"

Nick turned, looked at her, and replied solemnly, "I don't know. It's not getting any better."

Six months later, these initial frustrations would become too much for Nick. Despite wanting to succeed and being more than capable of doing so, Nick would end up resigning. He told his boss Alex that he'd received an offer from another firm that he couldn't refuse, but the real reason was his frustration at not knowing how to succeed in the firm. He'd been looking for a new job for several months by the time he resigned because he knew it wouldn't get any better.

•

In my time in business, I've seen too many bosses like Alex lose promising employees like Nick. Over time, this has disastrous effects in terms of wasted resources, reduced productivity, and unrealised business outcomes – not to mention the stress and anguish it creates for both employees and managers.

I wrote this book because I don't want you to be like Nick's boss Alex. Instead, I want to equip you with the tools and knowledge you need to make your new hires valuable, productive, and effective team members – fast. By the end of this book, you will know exactly what to do to help each new hire succeed in their new role. You will comprehend the staggering cost of ineffective onboarding and how to fix it. This book will provide you with a practical and straightforward toolset for any manager in your business to ensure your next hire has the best chance of succeeding. And if you've hired the wrong person, you will find out quickly and be able to act much faster.

I've been helping leadership teams build great companies for over a dozen years. Before that, I was an entrepreneur in one way or another for more than fifteen years. During this time, I learned that the first and most important rule of building a great company is getting the right people in the right seats and doing the right things in the right way. Everything else you want to achieve, any strategy, project, mission, or initiative, will struggle to succeed if you don't get that first rule right. And so, when hiring is done well, it should get the right people in the right seats. But onboarding is the missing piece of the puzzle. Onboarding takes those right people who are in the right seat from hiring and gets them to do the right things in the right way.

I also realised that the first rule of building a great company presents many important questions for leaders and that most of those questions are answered with effective onboarding. Over many years, this led me to develop and evolve a process to enable managers to confidently ensure that any new hire is the right person, in the right seat, doing the right things in the right way. I call this the onboarding sprint plan, and I'll take you through it later in this book.

The more I used the onboarding sprint plan with the teams I worked with, the clearer I became about the cost of ineffective onboarding in all its forms. I felt compelled to write this book to help leaders understand the actual cost of ineffective onboarding and share my simple process to overcome the problem – thereby positively impacting both leaders' and new hires' productivity and happiness.

My research for this book was extensive. I surveyed more than 1,100 CEOs and hiring managers and interviewed fifteen leaders from across the globe. I wanted to understand what worked and didn't work for them. I also reviewed as many books, articles, and interviews about onboarding as I could find to get an aggregated view of the best practices. I'll share this research with you throughout this book.

In my first book, *Made to Thrive: The Five Roles to Evolve Beyond Your Leadership Comfort Zone*, I asked, "What's the difference between a good leader and a great leader?" In this book, I ask, "How can we reduce onboarding debt and make new hires more effective, faster?"

I owe a debt of gratitude to the many people who have helped me with this book, each in their own way. I want to thank the following: Bev Attfield, Tim Clarkson, Mike Edmiston, Sandra Francis, Briony Freeman, Sam Hyder, Ian Judson, Josh Gardner, Matt Kuttler, Mike Mirau, David Metcalf, Chris Nichols, Srikanth Seshadri, Adam Siegal, Shannon Susko, Jess Temby, Jeremy Trumble, Garth Wardle, and Tristan White. I'd also like to thank all 1,109 CEOs and hiring managers who participated in the survey and provided the background for me to validate some of my concepts and, at times, disprove other ideas I had! I'd also like to make a special mention to my friend Kevin Lawrence who hosts a weekly podcast with me and has been a valuable sounding board for some of the work on this book.

Finally, I ask forgiveness from all those who have helped me with this book that I haven't mentioned above.

•

I will begin the book by defining onboarding and explaining the critical onboarding milestones and why they matter. Next, I will explain how most companies complete their onboarding process well before they gain any meaningful impact and how you can create a competitive difference for your organisation using onboarding.

I'll explain how the mindset most managers have towards hiring works against the outcomes they really want. Then I will introduce the concept of onboarding debt, similar to sleep debt, where over time, the accrued debt from ineffective onboarding creates a set of serious second-order consequences. Of course, this is what you *don't* want to happen in your firm.

Then, I will outline the connection between onboarding and culture, including the terrible cost that inadequate onboarding brings to a firm's culture and the hard dollar cost of ineffective onboarding. Next, I'll give you some simple tools to help you calculate how much ineffective onboarding is costing you. I'll also explain why onboarding can only be described as effective if it exits some new hires.

Having made the case for the importance of onboarding, I will then explain how to use the two tools in this book. I'll start with the role scorecard, which establishes the parameters of a new hire's success before they start. I'll then share the onboarding sprint plan, which will take the new hire through the three essential onboarding stages.

Finally, you will learn to use an onboarding sprint plan with the new hire during a weekly onboarding meeting. I'll share why you should use onboarding buddies and the importance of formally closing the onboarding process.

Let's get started.

CHAPTER 1

What is Onboarding?

Defining Onboarding

Onboarding is not hiring. It's not induction. It's not orientation, and it's not training.

Onboarding is the process of taking someone from outside your organisation and making them a productive, independent, and confident member of your team who understands the culture, the technical and process expectations, and your expectations as their manager.

The onboarding period begins when a person has signed a contract to work in your organisation and ends when they are a useful, valuable member of the team.

When designed correctly and consciously, your onboarding process should help create the type of culture you want to build or have built, and it should activate pride in the new employee as a valued member of the team.

Let's define some of the processes adjacent to onboarding.

Induction is where you admit a new employee to an organisation or role. It's like a licence to operate; it provides the employee the ability to participate in the organisation. You might classify a new hire as having been inducted when they have completed the forms to get paid and pay taxes, know their computer login and how to access their email, and have been issued security access cards.

Orientation is the process of helping a person become familiar with a location or situation. It is how they come to know their way around. After a new hire has completed orientation, they should know the location of the IT and HR departments and who to talk with if they need help. They should also know emergency procedures and the locations of the exits and restrooms. Orientation might also include things like car parking arrangements or an explanation of the org chart and who does what.

Training is where you teach an employee a new skill or behaviour or help them to improve an existing one. Training applies both to existing employees and new hires during the onboarding process. Once trained on a subject, new hires within the onboarding process should understand the processes and systems required to do their job. Or, to put it another way, they should understand "the way we do things here."

Induction, orientation, and training should form part of an effective onboarding process.

Ideally, an onboarding process should align with the statutory probation period for your country. In other words, you want the onboarding process to confidently tell you the person should stay or go within the legal probation period.

While Nick, who we met in the introduction, might have been inducted and been through orientation and perhaps even training, he didn't understand how to succeed. The induction, orientation, and training processes provided enough to get him started but not enough to succeed. He couldn't find what he needed, systems didn't make sense, and he didn't have enough time with his manager to ask questions. As a result, his manager and the organisation lost at least six months of productivity when Nick resigned. Team morale took a nosedive, the culture was threatened, and Nick and Alex experienced far more stress and turmoil than was necessary.

Every time a new person joins a team, the team fundamentally reinvents itself. As I said earlier, for a team to be effective, each person should be a productive, independent, and confident member of it. They must understand the culture, the technical and process expectations, and your expectations as their manager. If you have already achieved that within your team and hire a new person to join you, the entire team is impacted. The onboarding process – if it is carried out thoughtfully and systematically – reduces that impact.

Most countries have a three-to-six-month statutory limit on a probation period, after which standard employment legislation commences.

Let's now define a few other terms.

Candidate – Someone who has not yet signed an employment contract and is being considered for a role.

New hire – A person who has signed an employment contract and is a potential fit with the organisation, but until the end of the onboarding process, hasn't yet proven to be a successful fit.

Recent hire – A person who has signed an employment contract and completed the onboarding process, proving themselves as a successful fit.

Onboarding sprint plan – Built by the new hire's manager before advertising for the role, outlines the new hire's milestones to finish the onboarding process.

For better context, let's view these terms along a timeline of the onboarding process. See Figure 1.1:

Figure 1.1 **Onboarding process terminology**

Each team member should be a productive, independent, and confident contributor. They should understand the culture, the technical and process expectations, and your expectations. If you have already achieved that within a team and then hire a new person, the entire team's effectiveness is impacted. The onboarding process should reduce that impact.

Why a 90-Day Onboarding Process Matters

If there's one thing I can guarantee, it's that many of you are reading this and thinking, *"But I want to get my employee productive and MAKING MONEY as soon as possible. I don't have time for all this stuff."*

I'm not suggesting that new hires spend 100 percent of their time in those first months performing onboarding training, nor that you spend all your time teaching them.

You need to realise a return on investment as soon as possible. Still, unless your employees understand how to be productive in your organisation, which can take some effort and time, they will not be anywhere near as productive as they could be.

As Mike Mirau, CEO and Founder of Tribute Printing, said, *"The average person takes six months to be fully productive, but good onboarding can cut that in half – down to 90 days."*

If you think you don't have time for a 90-day onboarding process, consider this: Mike also wants his new hire MAKING MONEY as soon as possible, just like you. However, he recognises that the end goal is for the new hire to be not just productive but "fully productive." It's such a slight difference in mindset, but it can make all the difference in terms of your new hire grasping essential things about their new role, your expectations, and the company. The difference between what they know and what they *should* know at the end of onboarding is what I call *onboarding debt*, which I will explain in Chapter 2.

In my research for this book, I surveyed over 1,100 CEOs and hiring managers globally, across a range of organisations from less than ten employees to greater than five hundred employees. I asked many questions, including whether respondents agree or disagree with the following three statements that help define a successful onboarding:

- *After completing our onboarding process, new hires understand most of their manager's expectations.*

- *After completing our onboarding process, new hires understand most of our company culture.*

- *After completing our onboarding process, new hires understand most of our company processes.*

I compared the average of these three responses with the length of the respondent's onboarding process. This comparison, demonstrated in Figure 1.2, showed that the longer the onboarding process, the more likely it is that a recent hire will understand the manager's expectations, the culture, and the company processes.

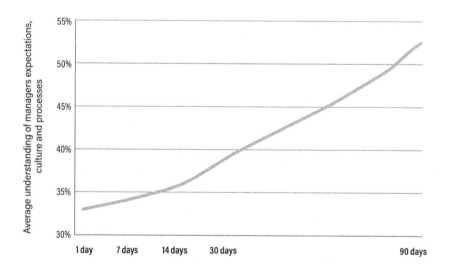

Figure 1.2 **Longer onboarding leads to a better understanding of expectations and processes**

As you can see, when an onboarding process lasts for a week or less, about 34 percent of respondents agree that once complete, their onboarding process leads to recent hires understanding the manager's expectations, the culture, and the company processes.

Yet if the onboarding process takes 90 days, about 53 percent of respondents agree that once complete, their onboarding process leads to recent hires understanding the manager's expectations, the culture, and the company processes.

This difference of around 19 percent is just one example of onboarding debt – an absence of understanding in the recent hire.

Perhaps you're wondering about the types of companies I surveyed and whether they were large or small. In Figure 1.3, you can see five segments ranging from less than ten employees to greater than five hundred employees. Respondents are divided between them.

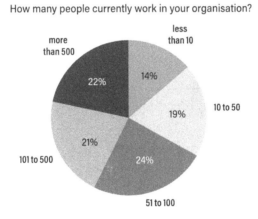

Figure 1.3 **Survey respondent company size**

My research found that most companies surveyed – 96 percent – have an onboarding process shorter than the recommended 90 days. As you can see in Figure 1.4, about 39 percent of companies surveyed have a seven-day process, and about 34 percent have a 14-day process. In total, 83 percent of respondents had an onboarding process of 14 days or less.

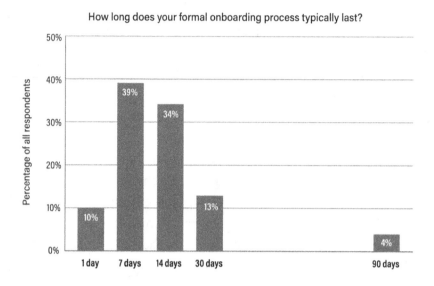

Figure 1.4 **Onboarding time as a percentage of total respondents**

When we overlay Figure 1.3 and Figure 1.4, as shown in Figure 1.5, we see that 83 percent of recent hires undergo an onboarding process of 14 days or less. Yet, the new hire's understanding of the manager's expectations, the culture, and the company processes only begins to improve at 30 days and continues to improve through to 90 days.

This graph is a powerful indictment of the current global process of onboarding. Most respondents to my survey had a seven-day onboarding process – yet the real impact of onboarding begins to accelerate after 30 days. If employees' onboardings do not progress past 30 days – and it's clear from my research that most don't – those employees are missing out on the opportunity to become fully effective in their roles. Their managers, and the organisations they belong to, can't possibly expect to have teams with a healthy and productive culture. This is why Nick felt so despondent on that day in the kitchen. He had not been made to feel that he was a valued member of his team – let alone understand the crucial aspects of his role in the company.

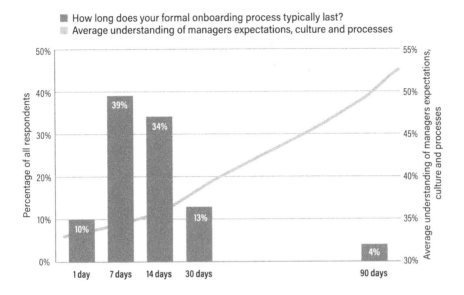

Figure 1.5 **Recent hire understanding compared to the percentage of total onboarding time for all respondents**

According to my research, as shown in Figure 1.5, employers are most likely to have a 7-day onboarding process. Only 34 percent of employers with a 7-day onboarding process agree that new hires understand their managers' expectations, the cultural expectations, and the technical and process expectations. However, 53 percent of employers with a 90-day onboarding process agreed with the same question.

Implementing a 90-day onboarding process should be a priority for you and your organisation.

Let's say your competitors have a 7-or-14-day onboarding process – as illustrated in Figure 1.5 – yet the real impact of onboarding begins to accelerate after 30 days through to 90 days. Could this create a strategic advantage for you? If your employees' understanding is significantly higher than your competitors' employees, how different would your firm be from competitors after a few years and perhaps tens or hundreds of hires? This gap also impacts other existing workers in the firm. If not taught during onboarding, there are so many things that your recent hires will never understand, and you will never find the time to teach them. Most managers act as if their employees might absorb key concepts via osmosis.

This is the terrible ongoing legacy of onboarding debt.

Yet, there is another aspect to consider.

A key outcome of onboarding is that you must be confident that the new hire is the right person for the role. If they are not the right person, you should know by the end of the process. If you have a 7-day onboarding process, then 83 days later, when the new hire's legal probation status has likely changed, you simply won't have anywhere near the same level of confidence in the person's fit. Because for the past 83 days, you've probably let them get on with the job!

Ideally, your onboarding process should align with the statutory probation period for your country. In other words, you want the onboarding process to enable you to confidently know whether the person should stay or go within the legal probation period. If they must go, it should cost you as little as possible and cause the least damage to your culture while complying with the law. Most countries have a three-to-six-month statutory limit on a probation period, after which standard employment legislation commences.[1]

Of course, you should seek advice from an employment expert in your region, but for the purpose of this book, we're working on 90 days, which is quite common across the world. The rigour of the 90-day onboarding process I describe in this book will give you absolute confidence about whether you need to exit the person within the legal time frame and begin the hiring process again.

I recently worked with a CEO who applied the onboarding process outlined in this book when hiring an operations manager. After six weeks, she was confident that the person was wrong, and the person left. Without this

---

1 https://www.dlapiperintelligence.com/goingglobal/employment/index.
html?t=06-employment-contracts

onboarding process, she said it would have taken nine months and great expense to figure out he was an unsuccessful fit.

The Binary Fit Fallacy

Let's consider what happens when a leader reflects on a recent new hire that has gone badly, resulting in that person exiting the company. The leader might explain the exit by saying, "The person was a bad fit." "How do you know?" one might ask. "They didn't fit," the leader replies. "But why?" the other person presses. "We know they didn't fit because they don't work here anymore!" the leader answers.

The actual reason for the person's departure is never uncovered in this conversation.

Now let's consider another situation where a person who was hired recently still works at the firm. "They were a good fit," the leader might explain. "How do you know?" their co-worker asks. The leader might then say, "Because they still work here!"

In both cases, the leader is likely considering the individual a good or bad fit *before* they start working for the organisation. They do not understand the most important aspect of hiring: when you hire someone, you're provided with a person who is a *potential* fit with your organisation. Then the onboarding process takes them from a potential fit to a successful fit or an unsuccessful fit.

Let's go back to the definition of onboarding. Onboarding is the process of taking someone from outside your organisation and making them a productive, independent, and confident member of your team who understands the culture, the technical and process expectations, and your expectations as their manager.

That definition results in a successful fit or an unsuccessful fit. It doesn't result in a good or bad fit.

Fit is not binary.
Fit is a spectrum.

When we think about fit as being binary – that a recent hire will not work out if they're not the right person – we are indoctrinating our teams with the tyranny of low expectations.

A binary fit mindset advocates that it is pointless to follow an onboarding process and give new hires a better understanding of the organisation – they'll either fit due to who they are, or they won't. We're saying that once the employment contract is signed, there is nothing we can do to increase the new hire's chance of success in their role. If the person is a bad fit, it's on them, and we're not responsible. The worst part about this is that it excuses poor onboarding practises because the manager has an excuse already prepared – the person just "wasn't a good fit." This excuse allows managers to shirk responsibility for spending time with their new hires.

You might hear leaders saying things like, "We've had such a bad run with hiring people," or "We're so unlucky with hiring," or "There are no decent candidates in our industry or geography or market."

It's like they're caught in a vicious loop where they say to themselves, "That former employee was a bad fit; any time spent with them would have been a complete waste. Therefore, we should not spend time with this other new hire in case they too are a bad fit because that would also be wasted time. Anyway, if they are going to work out well, we shouldn't need to spend time with them because they are a good fit."

To think that a person is a pre-determined good or bad fit is to discount the importance of the onboarding process and its purpose: to make your new hire a productive, independent, and confident member of your team or to confidently validate their exit.

To break this binary fit loop, instead of thinking about people as a good fit or a bad fit, which implies their success is entirely out of your control, I recommend using the phrases *successful fit* and *unsuccessful fit*. These phrases indicate that your onboarding process has validated whether the person is a successful fit. This represents a spectrum mindset.

Figure 1.6 illustrates the distinction between the binary mindset and the spectrum mindset. The binary mindset thinks that a bad fit definitely won't work and that a good fit definitely will work. On the other hand, with a spectrum mindset, all recent hires are on the spectrum between definitely will work through to definitely won't work. The onboarding process validates whether they are a successful or an unsuccessful fit.

Between contract signing and completing the onboarding process, a person must have the status of *potential fit*. After the onboarding process, their status changes to "successful fit," or they exit with the status of an "unsuccessful fit."

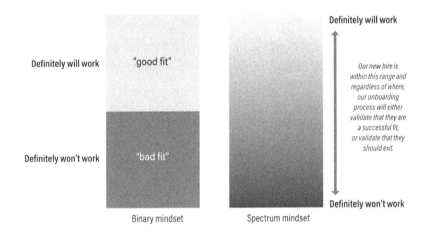

Figure 1.6 **Binary vs. spectrum mindset**

Therefore, as shown in Figure 1.7, the only way a leader can achieve a successful or unsuccessful fit with a spectrum mindset is via the onboarding process. Yet most managers will look at the left side of Figure 1.7, where we're bringing in a new hire without the need for the onboarding process, and think, "Rather than starting a new process, can't I just hire in a way that guarantees I'll get "good fit" staff in the first place?"

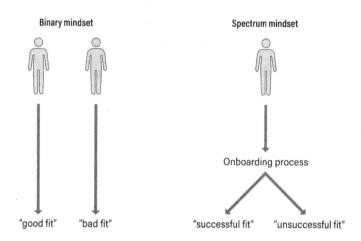

Figure 1.7 **The onboarding process is the only way to determine a successful or unsuccessful fit**

Before I answer that question, we must consider the cost of having an ineffective onboarding process. That's what I'm going to explain in Chapter Two: the enormous cost of not having an effective onboarding process and how the absence of this one simple process can significantly damage your business's productivity, retention, and culture.

Key Points

- *Every time a new person joins a team, the team fundamentally reinvents itself.*

- *The longer the onboarding process, the more a recent hire is likely to understand the managers' expectations, the culture, and the company processes.*

- *Around 83% of organisations have an onboarding process of 14 days or less, with almost 50% less than 7 days, yet the real impact of onboarding occurs between 30 and 90 days*

- *Onboarding is the only way to determine a successful versus an unsuccessful fit.*

- *An effective onboarding process reduces the burden or liability permanently carried into the team. It means the difference between what new hires should know and what they do know, which I call Onboarding Debt.*

CHAPTER 2

Onboarding Debt

Liability from a Lack of Understanding

On the day your new hire joins your team, they don't understand what is expected of them. They don't know that much about the culture. They don't understand the processes you use, and they may not be adept at some of the technical aspects of their role. Most of all, they don't know your expectations as their manager. And because they don't understand these things, they will solve problems on their own. They will do things the way they think is right, or they will do things they shouldn't, or they will neglect to do the things they should.

It's not your new hire's job to magically understand what's expected of them; it's your job to help them understand.

In my book *Made to Thrive,* I give leaders three key questions to assess an employee's potential to succeed in a role:

1 *Are they capable of succeeding in the role?*

2 *Do they understand what it takes to succeed in the role?*

3 *Do they want to succeed in the role?*

Whether they are capable and whether they want to succeed is on them. But whether new hires understand how to succeed is on you.

According to Gallup, only 12 percent of employees believe their company did a good job onboarding them. And from my research, they could be right.[2] My research tells a similar story. Managers are failing woefully in their job of helping new hires understand how to succeed, leading to out-of-control onboarding debt.

---

2 https://www.gallup.com/workplace/238085/state-american-workplace-report-2017.aspx

Onboarding debt is much like sleep debt. If you don't have enough sleep for a few nights, it's probably okay, but if you don't get enough sleep over weeks, months, and years, you accumulate a sleep debt, which can create serious health issues. Onboarding debt works in a similar way. The first moment of the first day a person joins your team, they carry the maximum amount of onboarding debt. Your job is to oversee a system that reduces that onboarding debt as effectively as possible. You must help them understand the culture, the technical and process expectations, and your expectations. If they don't understand and continue to work in your organisation into the future, there will be a difference between what they should know and what they know. This difference, this liability, is carried around like an invisible sack of stones on the back of every employee. It affects three main areas: productivity, retention, and the business's culture.

To what degree does onboarding affect these three areas? We'll look at culture in a moment, but first, the employee review website Glassdoor found that organisations with a strong onboarding process improve new hire retention by 82 percent and productivity by over 70 percent.[3]

In my research, I asked about attrition, which measures the number of people who exit organisations. The data I gathered provided a similar conclusion to Glassdoor. The longer an onboarding process, the more likely people are to know that it impacts the attrition rate, as shown in Figure 2.1.

As to how onboarding affects culture, I found that managers with a 90-day onboarding process were more than twice as likely as others to agree that new hires understand most of their company culture after the onboarding process, as shown in Figure 2.2.
In addition to asking respondents about their understanding of culture, I asked them about their understanding of managers' expectations and company processes.

As illustrated in Figure 2.3, the length of an onboarding process impacts a new hire's understanding across these three areas by an approximate 14 percent increase from the 30-day to 90-day processes. This is in

---

3 https://b2b-assets.glassdoor.com/the-true-cost-of-a-bad-hire.pdf

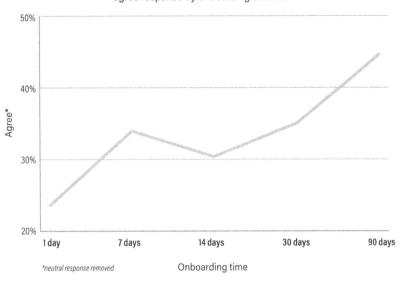

Figure 2.1 **Longer onboarding affects attrition rate**

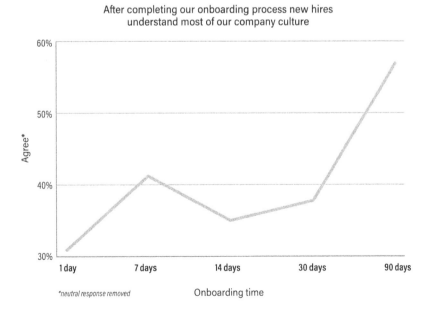

Figure 2.2 **Longer onboarding affects culture**

keeping with much of my research findings: the most significant impacts occur after 30-day processes, yet – as we learned in Chapter 1 – 83 percent of respondents had onboarding processes of 14 days or less.

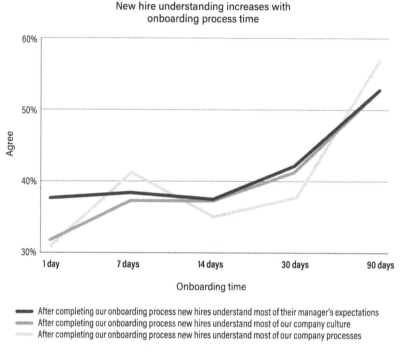

Figure 2.3 **Impact of onboarding process time on new hire understanding**

Let's now consider productivity.

Productivity can be defined as "the effectiveness of useful effort." To assess the impact of onboarding on a recent hire's effectiveness, we need to assume that most new hires will report to a manager, work within a team of co-workers with whom they will regularly interact, and work within a set of established company processes. Productivity, therefore, will be impacted by the way new hires fit within these areas.

To understand the value and impact of a successful onboarding process, we can consider the three critical elements to successful onboarding that we identified in Chapter 1. An onboarding process must accomplish these three outcomes, as illustrated in Figure 2.4.

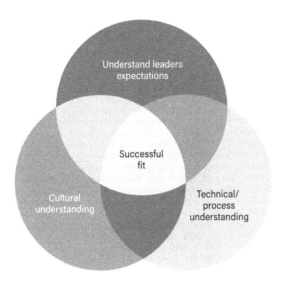

Figure 2.4 **Critical elements to successful onboarding.**

Let's think more deeply about these three critical elements of onboarding and their interdependence. We're all familiar with the international symbol for "play," which is commonly used on music and video players – as shown in Figure 2.05. This symbol indicates *starting* something. In the context of this book, it represents how we effectively start new hires.

Figure 2.5 **Symbol for play – indicating starting something**

Next, we take the triangle and add the three onboarding elements to each point, as shown in Figure 2.6.

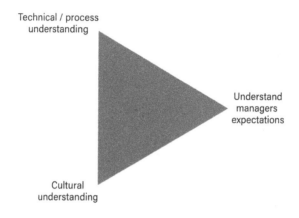

Figure 2.6 **The three onboarding elements overlayed on the play symbol**

So, for a recent hire to "play" at your organisation, for them to successfully onboard, there are three elements that you as a leader must ensure to avoid excessive onboarding debt. If any one of the elements is missing or very weak, the new hire won't complete their onboarding as a successful fit.

If a recent hire understands their managers' expectations and technical processes but doesn't understand the culture, they won't complete their onboarding as a successful fit.

If a recent hire understands the culture and their managers' expectations but doesn't understand the technical processes, they won't complete their onboarding and become a successful fit.

Finally, if a recent hire understands the culture and technical processes but doesn't understand their managers' expectations, they won't complete their onboarding as a successful fit.

When a person signs a contract to join your company, they don't understand any of these three elements within your organisation. Perhaps their previous skills or experience will help in this role, but there is no validation of this yet on their first day. Without that validation, when they've only just agreed to come and work with your firm, they likely will not understand your expectations, the culture, or the processes you use. You would understandably rate them a zero out of ten across all three dimensions, as illustrated in Figure 2.7.

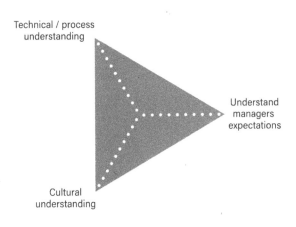

Figure 2.7 **Sample onboarding assessment – Day 1**

If, 90 days later, you are asked to rate your score out of ten on how well the new hire understands these three elements relative to their time spent with the firm, you might give your response as:

- *Understand manager's expectations – 6/10*

- *Understand company culture – 6/10*

- *Understand technical/processes – 7/10*

This will allow you to calculate that your new hire understands about 63 percent of what they should after 90 days and, importantly, that they do not understand about 37 percent. This lack of understanding across these three elements is the new hire's onboarding debt, as illustrated in Figure 2.8.

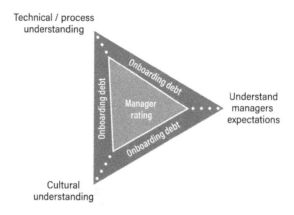

Figure 2.8 **Sample onboarding assessment – Day 90**

Imagine if an electronic map didn't understand 37 percent of the roads in your city. You would take it back to where you bought it, right? If the new hire doesn't understand 37 percent of what they need to after 90 days, should you exit them from the business?

Regardless, you must assess whether it is the new hire's fault or whether an ineffective onboarding process might be to blame.

Skipping an effective onboarding process is like borrowing money. With borrowed money, you can do something sooner than you could otherwise, but it comes at the cost of interest.

Reduced productivity is the ongoing cost of not having an effective onboarding process, much like the interest you pay when you borrow money.

Reduced productivity results from people misunderstanding the company culture, their manager's expectations, or the role's technical processes. When this happens, they do things the wrong way or in a less effective way. Efficiencies are lost, costly mistakes are made, and work must be re-done.

When you accumulate too much financial debt, most of your effort ends up simply servicing the debt. In the same way, if you accumulate too much onboarding debt within your team without reducing it, you spend most of your effort addressing embedded misunderstandings and their consequences.

Misunderstanding Multiplied by Complexity

When a single hire is onboarded poorly, onboarding debt accrues. This is significant in terms of the potential productivity we miss out on for that individual. But teams are complex, and we must also factor in the debt generated for all team members because of that new hire and the ways they interact, and any existing onboarding debt that other team members may carry.

If there are two people in a team, there are only two points of communication – my interaction with you and your interaction with me. If there are three people, there are six points. Add just one more person and take that number to four people in a team, and there are twelve points of communication, as shown in Figure 2.9.

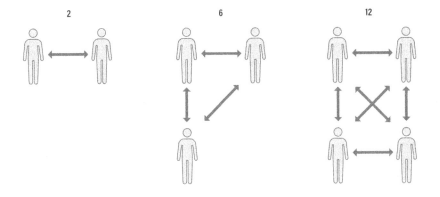

Figure 2.9 **Points of communication for different team sizes**

This increasing complexity makes the onboarding debt ever more expensive to service. For example, suppose you have a team with each person carrying an onboarding debt of 37 percent. This complexity across different communication channels grows exponentially, and the debt is incurred much faster than the team's growth.

To understand this increasing complexity within a team, we can use the formula C(C-1). C represents the communication points, with each communication point equally being a point of complexity, as shown in Figure 2.10.

For a four-person team, the points of complexity are (4-1) x 4 = 12
For an eight-person team, the points of complexity are (8-1) x 8 = 56
For a 12-person team, the points of complexity are (12-1) x 12 = 132

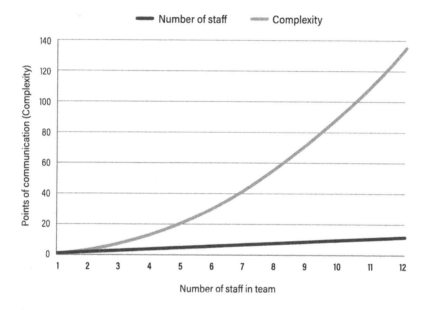

Figure 2.10 Increasing complexity in a growing team

Jeff Bezos understood this as he scaled Amazon and introduced the "two-pizza rule." As Brad Stone, author of *The Everything Store*, noted:

> "The entire company would restructure itself around what he called 'two-pizza teams.' Employees would be organised into autonomous groups of fewer than ten people — small enough that, when working late, the team members could be fed with two pizza pies."

If we refer to Figure 2.11, we can see how individual onboarding debt impacts team onboarding debt. With a team of two, if person A understands 80 percent of the culture, their manager's expectations, and technical and process expectations, and person B understands 50 percent, then the team's average understanding is 80 + 50 / 2 = 65 percent. Therefore, they have a team onboarding debt of 35 percent. But this is only multiplied through two points of communication.

With a team of three, if person A has a 35 percent understanding, person B has 60 percent, and person C has 85 percent, then the average team understanding is 60 percent, and the onboarding debt is 40 percent. Remember, the misunderstanding can occur anywhere within six points of communication in a team of three. The presence of a top performer in this team doesn't override the risk of issues arising from misunderstanding.

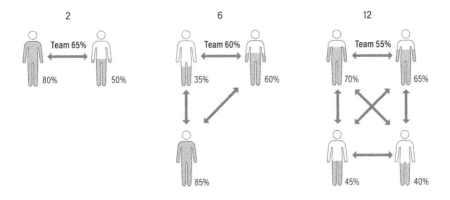

Figure 2.11 Team onboarding debt as a team grows

As we grow our teams, the individual onboarding debt remains. People find workarounds, learn lessons, and figure things out, so the individual debt brought into a team will fade beyond their initial 90 days, but people's bad habits will become entrenched.

I've asked many leaders, *"How well does that person understand your expectations on a scale of one to ten?"* In some cases, employees who've been in the role for many years only score a four. Just because a person has been in a position for a long time doesn't guarantee they completely understand the culture, their manager's expectations, or technical and process expectations. Of course, if a leader scores a long-term employee four, they are usually at the point where they can't decide what to do: whether to manage the person out of the business or not. That leader probably should have followed an effective onboarding process in the first place to have confidence within the first 90 days and ensure a successful fit if the person were to remain.

Suppose you find yourself in a situation where you are rating existing team members low on their understanding of your expectations. In that case, I'd suggest you consider the other two questions and rate them out of ten on the culture and technical and process expectations. Then you can begin to ask why you rated them in that manner and where they are deficient. Rather than viewing this as onboarding existing team members again, something I'm sure they might be upset about, view it as training. Consider the process outlined in Chapter 6: Preparing to Effectively Onboard, and how you could apply that principle to a training program that would reduce the overall onboarding debt.

The average score or misunderstanding for an individual and a team is important to consider, but the relationship between complexity and misunderstanding is also important. If you are rating a person out of ten across three elements – the culture, manager's expectations, and technical and process expectations – and multiply these, the maximum total score is 1000 (10 x 10 x 10 = 1,000). In the example above, the score was 6, 6, and 7, yielding a total score of 252.

When you multiply the three elements together, the multiplied onboarding score grows on a linear scale, whereas complexity increases exponentially.

As you grow a team, even if your onboarding process is perfect, if the manager rates new hires a ten out of ten every time, eventually, as the team grows, the complexity will catch up, as shown in Figure 2.12.

Think back to Jeff Bezos' two-pizza rule. No matter how good the team is or how good your processes are, eventually, the complexity, growing exponentially, will exceed the linear capability of a team's understanding.

The theoretical limit of a team, where complexity overrides their onboarding score, is ten people – incidentally, about the same as the number of people who could eat two pizzas.

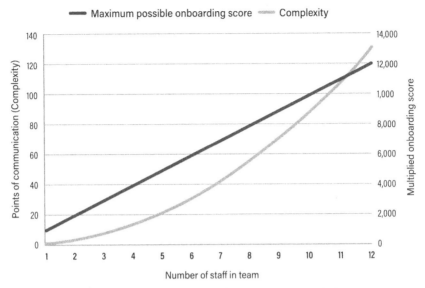

Figure 2.12 **Maximum possible onboarding score vs. team complexity**

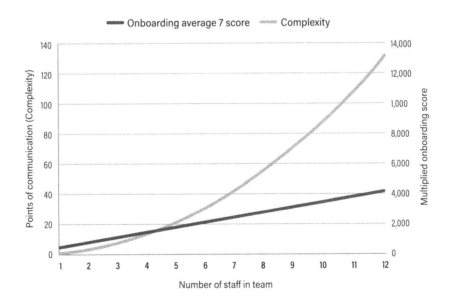

Figure 2.13 **Team onboarding average 7 score vs. complexity**

That's the theory, but what if, in the real world, you had an average team understanding of seven, as shown in Figure 2.13? And let's be fair, rating a new hire seven out of ten on their understanding isn't a bad score! But, with an average seven score, once you reach a team of four, the complexity exceeds the understanding. Breaking this threshold results in more errors, more issues, more rework, and lower productivity.

And so, if we're achieving a rating of seven out of ten for new hires, once you exceed a team of four, you will experience increasingly more problems as the team grows if you don't increase the onboarding scores. We can then consider comparing the average onboarding score of seven to the maximum score of ten, as shown in Figure 2.14. The difference between a score of seven and a score of ten represents onboarding debt.

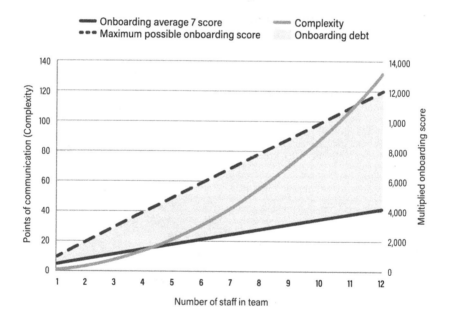

Figure 2.14 **Team onboarding average 7 score vs. maximum possible, demonstrating onboarding debt**

You may accrue onboarding debt through a single hire due to their misunderstanding. However, that misunderstanding is multiplied by the team's complexity. As a team grows, leaders must reduce the team's onboarding debt to deal with increased complexity if they wish to remain effective.

In the first chapter, I outlined the binary fit fallacy and how instead of viewing hires as a good or bad fit, it's important to view them as a potential fit during the onboarding process, after which they become a successful or an unsuccessful fit. Let's now look at how onboarding debt is accrued through the mindset of good and bad fit.

Accruing Onboarding Debt Through Good Fit

At the end of the onboarding process, you must know why the recent hire was successful or why they were unsuccessful.

An effective onboarding process is essential not only because you want to have productive, independent, and confident team members who understand the culture, manager's expectations, and technical and process expectations, but because you want to stop those who aren't going to succeed before they damage your culture or productivity any further.

If you don't know why it worked, how do you know that it did work?

If the only measure you have is that a recent hire is still employed, the only thing you know for sure is that they haven't yet left.

However, if you can specifically target precisely why they weren't a successful fit – for example, they didn't resonate with the values or didn't want to meet their manager's expectations – you create a legitimate reason to restart the hiring process. You avoid that person staying, not aligning with the core values, or perhaps not meeting their manager's expectations, thereby negatively impacting the productivity of the team.

If you have followed a best practice onboarding process and the new hire has stayed, you should be able to say, "We know why it worked."

If you have followed a best practice onboarding process and the new hire has left, you should be able to say, "We know why it didn't work."

Compare this to those who aren't following a best practice onboarding process in the onboarding success matrix in Figure 2.15.

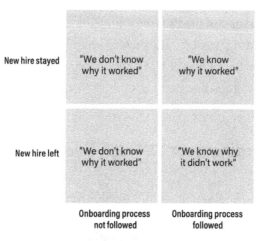

Figure 2.15 Onboarding success matrix

Now let's apply some definitions to each of the four areas in Figure 2.16. We want to be on the two right-hand quadrants of successful fit and unsuccessful fit. Remember that an unsuccessful fit is also a win, as you've protected the culture.

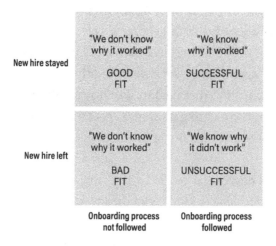

Figure 2.16 Onboarding success matrix with fit definitions

The difference between a good fit and a successful fit may seem very small at first. But a successful fit occurs because the organisation has caused the person to fit. Equally, if someone said to you that their recent hire was an unsuccessful fit rather than a bad fit, it implies that they tried to make them fit but couldn't. The process served its purpose.

The day you hire someone, they become a potential fit: there is a potential that they could fit well into the role they've been hired to perform. When you put that person through your onboarding process, you will know whether *you* are successful or unsuccessful in *your* attempt to have them fit *your* role.

If we look at Figure 2.17, we can see that a good fit is defined on the two-by-two matrix in the top left as the area where somebody did not follow the onboarding process and the new hire stayed. This would feel like a great success for many leaders: they've filled the role and did not waste time on an onboarding process or hiring a replacement who didn't work out. A good fit is where leaders might reluctantly say, "We don't know why it worked, but it did!" And this is where onboarding debt is accrued—you've traded the short-term gain of not spending time on the process for the long-term pain of their misunderstanding.

And so, the wrong people do what they think is right.

The right people do what they think is right.

And the people who could be the right people do what they think is right.

But there's a good chance that none of them are doing what you already know is right.

Across all the many facets of your company, this can add up to hundreds if not thousands of differences. This is onboarding debt (see Figure 2.17).

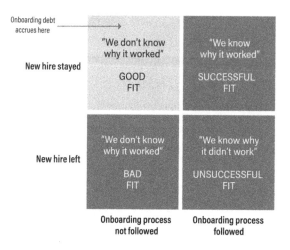

Figure 2.17 **Onboarding debt accrual**

They seem like a good fit – or at least they weren't a bad enough fit for you to go through the pain of exiting them.

But unless you know why a new hire has been successful, unless you can confidently rate their understanding, how do you know they will continue to be successful?

How will you know how their onboarding debt impacts the culture of their team?

That's what I'm going to explain in the next chapter: how well-meaning but inadequate onboarding processes inadvertently create bad cultures and how effective onboarding is the seed to growing a great culture.

Key Points

- *Onboarding debt is the liability that you incur with each new hire.*

- *The amount of debt you incur and retain depends on your onboarding process.*

- *More onboarding debt means a less successful team.*

- *You must know why a new hire is successful or not successful to avoid incurring onboarding debt.*

CHAPTER 3

Onboarding is the Seed to Growing a Great Culture

Connecting Onboarding Debt and Culture

How do companies inadvertently create bad cultures?

Many of today's thinkers and writers discuss how to identify if you have a bad culture and what to do about it. But few, if any, ask how bad cultures occur.

It's like there's a disease, and all the experts are talking about how to identify if you have the disease and what to do if you have it, but no one asks how one catches the disease in the first place.

This problem is so pervasive that a search for "what creates a bad culture" produced only two results on Google in 2021. But searching Google for signs of a bad culture without quotation marks produced 378 million results. I had to use quotation marks to be specific in the first search because all the results I could find without quotation marks only discussed the signs of a bad culture, not what causes it.

Before he died in 2005, *Businessweek* magazine labelled Peter Drucker as "the man who invented management." Drucker, who was undoubtedly one of the greatest business thinkers of the twentieth century, coined the phrase "Culture eats strategy for breakfast." This phrase means that no matter how good your strategic plan is, the effectiveness of your strategy will suffer if your company has a dysfunctional culture.

If a good culture is the foundation of success, then understanding the cause of bad cultures, not just the symptoms, is one of the most important things that a leader who seeks success must do.

Imagine you assembled a group of ten random people into a team. However, you provided no instruction, guidance, or training about the culture, technical and process expectations, and leader's expectations. What would be the resulting culture of the team in a few months or a few years? At best, it would be a roll of the dice.

Maybe you could get lucky, and it would be okay.

But more than likely, people would do what they think is right. They would try to do the right thing. But every one of the ten people's interpretations of the right thing, in any situation, could be different.

Those different perspectives can lead to misunderstandings and differences of opinion, and over time, those minor issues can compound and create a dysfunctional culture.

Now consider the opposite—a team of ten random people you provide with a detailed onboarding plan. Over 90 days, you help them understand, learn, apply, and then embed the cultural, technical, and process expectations and the leader's expectations to be a successful fit. Equally, those who are an unsuccessful fit depart after that 90-day onboarding.

The result is that the team who participated in the onboarding will understand what is right. There will be fewer misunderstandings and differences of opinion. There will be better communication about what the team agrees on and a much lower chance of a dysfunctional culture.

The higher the onboarding debt, the more likely an organisation will have cultural issues.

Think about the length of your onboarding process, and then consider that 49 percent of respondents I surveyed had a 7-day or less onboarding process, and 83 percent had 14-days or less of onboarding. The vast majority of onboarding processes are one or two weeks. That's five or ten working days to maximise understanding and minimise onboarding debt.

Reflecting on the high number of firms with shorter onboarding periods, consider that one of the questions I asked within my survey was whether respondents agreed or disagreed with the statement, "After completing their onboarding process, new hires understand most of our company culture." Survey respondents who disagreed with that statement were twenty-seven times more likely to disagree that "Our onboarding process positively contributes to our culture."

Also, it seems that formal, documented meetings to conclude an onboarding process positively connect with culture. Respondents who didn't complete their onboarding process with a formal documented meeting were forty-two times more likely to disagree that their onboarding process positively contributes to their culture than those who did.

Furthermore, those who agreed with the statement that their *onboarding process concludes with a formal, documented meeting with the new hire* were more than twice as likely to agree that their onboarding process positively contributes to their culture. We'll examine this topic in more detail in Chapter 7.

There is a direct connection between the onboarding process and the culture within an organisation.

In my research, 85 percent of respondents with a 90-day onboarding process agreed or somewhat agreed with the statement that *our onboarding process positively contributes to our culture*. Yet, as shown in Figure 3.1, that drops down to 50 percent for those with a one-day onboarding process.

People with a longer onboarding process are more likely to agree that it positively contributes to their culture.

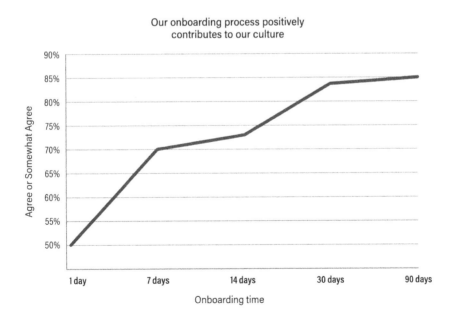

Figure 3.1 **Longer onboarding positively impacts culture**

But do people with shorter processes know what they're missing?

For the people with shorter processes who didn't agree or somewhat agreed that their onboarding process contributes to their culture, it wasn't at the expense of disagreement. No, those votes instead went to neutral responses. By not agreeing or disagreeing, respondents indicated that they don't know whether their onboarding process impacts their culture, as demonstrated in Figure 3.2.

It's one thing to say I agree and another thing to say I disagree, but a neutral response has a meaning all its own.

The shorter the onboarding process, the less likely people will know whether the onboarding process positively contributes to culture.

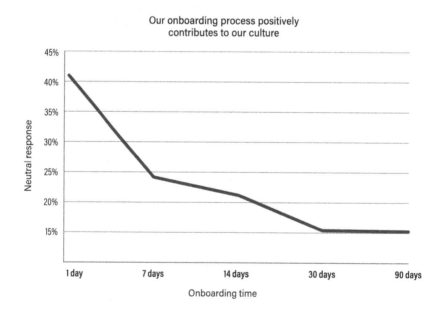

Figure 3.2 Longer onboarding leads to more confidence in the impact of the onboarding process on culture

Finally, in Figure 3.3, I add two other questions relating to culture and note how the neutral response changes. From this, we can conclude that shorter onboarding processes resulting in higher levels of onboarding debt led to:

- *Less understanding of how onboarding affects culture*

- *Less understanding whether after their onboarding, new hires understand the culture*

- *Less knowledge of whether hiring the wrong people affects culture*

The shorter the onboarding process, the less likely people will know whether onboarding contributes to the culture in any form whatsoever.

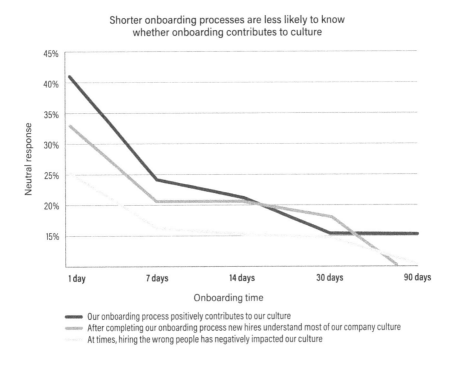

Figure 3.3 **Impact of shorter onboarding processes on understanding onboarding**

Identifying and fixing bad cultures might make for popular reading and lucrative consulting contracts, but the root cause is inadequate onboarding, and that is where any effort should begin.

Remedying poor onboarding ensures that recent hires are a successful fit and those recent hires who successfully fit are the only ones brought into the organisation.

An organisation with excessive onboarding debt has many areas of misunderstanding. That misunderstanding affects positive communication and negatively impacts culture.

The quality of your culture directly reflects the quality of your onboarding process.

Values + Behaviours + Onboarding = Great Culture

Every time a new person joins a team, the team becomes a new version of itself.

If you had a social basketball team playing evenings with four of your middle-aged friends, and one of those friends left and was replaced with Michael Jordan, you now have a new version of your team. Sure, your chances of winning have dramatically increased, but your new star recruit doesn't know the culture you and your friends enjoy. His expectations and commitment may be different. And his understanding of the technical and process aspects of the game is different from other team members. The team has been fundamentally reinvented because you have added one new member.

If you replace a single person in a work team consisting of seven people, that team is now a new version of itself. Is the new person loud or quiet? Do they have a high or low IQ? Are they aggressive or passive? Are they social or an introvert? The new person might only represent 14 percent of the team, but they create new dynamics across the entire team and how the team operates.

When you incur onboarding debt, that new version of the team, with all its misunderstanding, is the seed that grows into cultural problems.

There's a great irony here because employees already know this. As we've discussed in Chapter 1, Gallup found that only 12 percent of employ-ees strongly agree their organisation does a great job of onboarding new employees.[4] At the same time, Jenna Filipkowski from the Human Capital Institute identified that 58 percent of organisations say their onboarding program is focused on processes and paperwork.[5]

The induction process should have an administration and compliance focus.

The onboarding process should be structured and strategic, with a focus on people and understanding.

Leaders' best efforts to improve their company culture will be worthless if a new hire joins the team who is not a successful fit with the culture. Because when the team reinvents itself to incorporate this new team member, the new hire's onboarding debt will negate any leaders' improve-ments to the culture. That is why you must address the root cause of cultural issues before you address the culture itself.

Get your onboarding working well, and then improve your culture.

In my book *Made to Thrive*, I note, "If we look back to the origins of the word culture, it is derived from the Latin word 'colere' which means to care or to cultivate.

In the context of your role as a CEO, when it comes to culture, your job is to care for or cultivate your people."

I go on, "Imagine you are the custodian of each person you employ. Of course, eventually, every person will leave to get another job, so each person has a beginning, middle and end with you. As their custodian, during this time, how are you cultivating your people? How are you caring for them? After the end, will they look back on their time under your custodi-anship as good or great?"

---

4   https://www.gallup.com/workplace/238085/state-american-workplace-report-2017.aspx

5   https://www.hci.org/research/
talent-pulse-32-onboarding-outcomes-fulfill-new-hire-expectations

To apply that concept logically, one might suggest that the way to build a lousy culture is not to care or not cultivate your people.

And that's the key to successful onboarding. Managers are caring enough about new hires to spend time and build an onboarding plan to cultivate them. And with that insight, let's amend the statement above.

Get your managers caring about onboarding enough to spend the time and build an onboarding plan to cultivate new hires and then improve your culture.

Ask yourself and your managers, "How do you cultivate a new hire under your custodianship? What do you do in the first weeks or months to cultivate them?"

Over the past few decades, core values have emerged as a must-have for organisations. Unfortunately, many marketing firms have helped some people define these values, and these firms can pollute the original purpose of values by considering the values through the customer's eyes. It doesn't matter what the customer thinks about your values. In collective leadership, your values tell you who you are, good, bad, or ugly. Your values document your deeply held beliefs. These beliefs are bone-deep.

Values shine a light on that which is immovable, non-negotiable. Values should not be aspirational; they should be alive in the organisation today. They should be so deeply held that you would take a financial hit to maintain the integrity of a value.

If values tell us who we are and our deeply held beliefs, then having core values phrases alone is not sufficient for people to understand how we live those values.

For example, many people could interpret a core value entitled "Get it done" in many ways. Again, misunderstanding, as demonstrated through onboarding debt, would become an issue.

One person might interpret "Get it done" as getting it done at any cost. Another person might interpret it as getting it done as quickly as possible. And yet another might interpret it as getting it done and don't do anything else. Therefore, we need to have core values and behaviours that explain how we live those values.

Core Values explain who we are as collective leadership and our deeply held beliefs.

Behaviours explain how we live those values. If we execute the behaviours, we will live the core values.

Figure 3.4 illustrates how each core value, represented by the seat, is supported by a set of behaviours represented by the stool's legs.

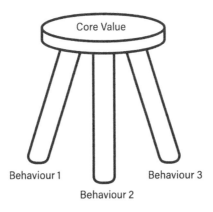

Figure 3.4 **A set of behaviours support each core value**

Tristan White, CEO at The Physio Co, a team I've worked with for many years and who have been recognised as a "Great Place to Work" for more than eleven consecutive years, has four core values:

- *Respect everyone*

- *Be memorable*

- *Find a better way*

- *Think big, act small*

Below is an example of "Be memorable" and its four supporting behaviours, which help team members understand what it means.

Be Memorable

- *We are friendly and make positive first impressions.*

- *We make people smile with our personal and understanding approach.*

- *We take the time to celebrate milestones and successes.*

- *We wow people whenever possible.*

You can see how "Be memorable" might be interpreted in a certain manner for a reader. But, your interpretation of "Be memorable" as a simple phrase could be different from my interpretation, which could also be different from Tristan's interpretation. Yet, when we read a core value and how it is defined through the behaviours, there is a lot less opportunity for misunderstanding. If we want to understand the culture at The Physio Co, it's important that we know the core values and how they are defined through behavioural expectations.

If you have five core values and four behaviours describing each core value, you will have a total of twenty behaviours. And those twenty behaviours should accurately describe your culture. If you had all the values and behaviours written on a wall, a simple test might be, does that series of statements accurately, completely articulate our culture? It should. Your values and behaviours should be a watertight, verbal description of your culture.

Therefore, values + behaviours = culture.

If you have been able to articulate your culture in this manner, if you can confidently say that your list of values and subsequent behaviours accurately capture your culture and how you cultivate and care for your people, then consider the complexity and nuances across all these behaviours and values. Also, consider all the stories of what your team has done and not done relative to each one. There could be perhaps three stories about each behaviour. If, for example, we asked Tristan about his behaviour of "We take the time to celebrate milestones and successes," he could very easily provide a few stories that help us understand what to do and what not to do regarding that behaviour. These stories will then enable us to understand the behaviour at an even deeper level. Back to our example, we have five values, four behaviours, and three stories about each behaviour. We could now have sixty stories to tell to help people completely understand the culture.

I don't think any leader would want to sit down and discuss sixty stories about behaviours and how they connect to values in one sitting. Equally, new hires would be nodding asleep. Also, as I discuss in the next chapter, new hires simply won't remember what you tell them in one sitting. And so, we need to build an understanding of the values, behaviours, and stories over time. Sixty stories, as indicated above, and a 90-day onboarding meeting once per week, averages out to around four or five stories per meeting—a more achievable practice.

Unless you help new hires really understand the values and the behaviours that support them, the misunderstanding that presents as onboarding debt will prevent you from building a great culture. Onboarding is how you use values and behaviours to address the root cause of a bad culture.

Let's look at Figure 3.5. We can think of the effort made by a firm like a fruit tree, where a great culture is the fruit we are hoping to harvest. Core values are present in a great culture but don't produce a great culture. Core values and behaviours are better than just core values but are still not enough to produce a great culture. However, when you put the core values and the behaviours together with an effective onboarding, you can produce the fruit you're seeking, which is a great culture.

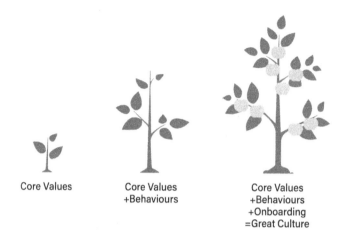

Figure 3.5 **Core values, behaviours, and onboarding contribute to a great culture**

Activating Pride Within Onboarding

There's a moment when a person signs an employment contract, and several of your worries lift from your shoulders.

"I've solved that problem," you may think, "I've got a person in that role. Let's see how they work out."

But that's not what the new hire is thinking.

They're probably thinking, "I've solved that problem, I've secured that role; let's see how this new employer works out."

According to a survey by the Aberdeen Group, 87 percent of new employees aren't fully committed to a new job for the first six months[6]. A further study by BambooHR revealed that the average company loses one in six of its new hires each month for the first three months[7].

Just because you've hired someone into a role, there is no evidence that they are committed to you or will stay. In fact, the onus is now on you as

---

6   https://www.bamboohr.com/resources/ebooks/guide-to-onboarding/

7   https://www.bamboohr.com/resources/ebooks/guide-to-onboarding/

their manager to increase their engagement, their connection to the team and the firm, and to activate their pride. Remember, they were probably speaking with other potential employers only a few weeks ago.

Let's consider the onboarding period from two perspectives: the manager's point of view and the new hire's point of view.

	Manager's point of view	New hire's point of view
Employment contract signed	Is all the paperwork in order? How can we get this new hire up to speed as quickly as possible?	Is this the right job for me? Is this the right company for me? Is the contract as expected?
Two weeks before the start day	Is everything organised for the new hire's first day? Computer, paperwork, meetings with HR booked? How can we get this new hire up to speed as quickly as possible? Does the new hire know about the workplace rules and regulations?	What will it be like to work with my new manager? What will my new job involve? What are my co-workers like? I wonder what will happen on my first day?
Start day	Does the new hire have all the right resources to do their job? Are we making a good impression?	Will I get a warm welcome? Maybe I will meet a friend or get a welcome pack? Perhaps even a morning tea to welcome me?
First week	Is the paperwork complete? Is everyone following the onboarding process?	Does my manager care about me? Do I know who to talk to if there's an issue? Have I made the right decision?
First month	Is the new hire settling in? Are there any issues that need resolving?	Am I actively contributing to the business? Do I understand what is expected of me? Do I know where to go with any unresolved issues?
Second month	Is the new hire productive and contributing to the organisation?	How can I do better in my job? How can I make this role mine? Do I have a best friend at work?
Third month	Is the new hire a productive, useful, and valuable member of the team?	Do I love my job? Can I keep learning and growing in this company? Can I see myself here in two years? Can I do my best work here?

Table 3.1 **Managers view compared to the new hires view**

When a new hire signs a contract and the recruiting phase has concluded, your firm enters a trial period with them in their mind for up to six months. If your recruiting process has worked well and produced a potential fit, you must understand that the new hire needs to successfully fit from both your perspective and their perspective through onboarding.

Once a person signs an employment contract, one of the essential tasks is activating and amplifying that person's pride. There are several touchpoints through onboarding where we can achieve this.

For Jeremy Trumble, Principal at FBT Architects in Albuquerque, New Mexico, developing their onboarding process and connecting it to the core values and culture has produced tangible results. Says Trumble, "About a week before the person is due to start, we bring them in for half a day so that their first day isn't really their first day. We're able to talk about things without pressure. They get to meet team members, and we normally have lunch together, so they are both comfortable and excited on the day they formally start."

"Then, after a few weeks, we meet with them and discuss the core values. We talk about how we established them, and what we do with them. We then tell them why we hired them based on those core values. You can see a real sense of pride when defining what we do and how they fit in. That's been our key to sinking hooks into a new employee right away.

We can teach anybody to draft but bringing somebody in who can hit the ground running and become a contributing member of the team is way more important if they get what we are trying to do here."

By explaining that they hired a person based on their core values, FBT Architects establish a bond with the new hire. They unlock a sense of pride in them toward both the team and the boss.

In my book *Made to Thrive*, I discuss the four prides of an employee. Employees must be:

Proud of their company
Proud of their team
Proud of their boss
Proud of their product

Or they will eventually leave.

One of the keys to successful onboarding is activating the new hire's pride. A team with a great culture has pride that begins during onboarding. On their first day, Apple employees receive this note[8]:

There's work, and there's your life's work.

The kind of work that has your fingerprints all over it. The kind of work that you'd never compromise on. That you'd sacrifice a weekend for. You can do that kind of work at Apple. People don't come here to play it safe. They come here to swim in the deep end.

They want their work to add up to something.

Something big. Something that couldn't happen anywhere else.

Welcome to Apple.

If you own a small or medium-sized business and give your employees that note, you may generate ridicule rather than pride. But there are still things you can do if you're in this situation. The objective in activating pride is to connect the story of the new hire to the company's story. The new hire should understand how their own story relates to the success of the company story.

We can also activate pride before new hires even begin. For Bev Attfield, Principal of Workplace Science at Jostle.me, ensuring new hires feel comfortable and supported on their first day sets the tone for the remainder of the relationship. Says Attfield, "About a week before they arrive, they get an email from their team lead with what to expect on their first day, what to do on their first day, and what their first day is going to look and feel like. We also send them all the technical invitations to get plugged in before they even start so they can become as engaged as they choose to. For remote employees, we adopt the same mindset, but have adapted our

8   https://www.loopinsight.com/2012/05/07/apples-welcome-letter/

behaviours to suit a virtual format. For example, day 1 starts with a video call with their team lead, followed by a series of calls that would mimic the in-person orientation."

Then Attfield describes the first-day experience for new hires. "On their first day in the office, their desk would be ready, and they would have swag on their desk with a welcome handwritten note from their team. After that, they would go out for a team lunch with their immediate team, and then they would get plugged in to all sorts of meetings throughout the day to help get them set up in our environment and things they need to do their job. So, we just try and make it as simple and focussed as possible to make sure that they don't need to absorb everything and need to know everything in the first day."

Pride is an essential consideration within onboarding because employees today look at jobs the same way consumers look at products. They are less likely to stay at a job simply because they get paid. In this world that values experiences so highly, people who sign up for an experience at a workplace and don't get it will soon be looking for other employers who will live up to their commitment. In the same manner that consumers become loyal to brands they connect with, who meet their promises, employees can become advocates for and proud of their employer.

Activating and amplifying the pride in new hires will help you build a better culture and reduce attrition. In the next chapter, we will discuss the price of that attrition and the other costs of inadequate onboarding.

Key Points

- *People with a longer onboarding process are more likely to agree that it positively contributes to their culture.*

- *The shorter the onboarding process, the less likely people can know whether onboarding contributes to culture.*

- *If a good culture is the foundation of success, then understanding the cause of bad cultures, not just the symptoms, is one of the most important things that a leader who seeks success must do.*

- *The higher the onboarding debt, the more likely an organisation will have cultural issues.*

- *Every time you add a new person to a team, you fundamentally reinvent that team.*

- *Leaders' best efforts to improve their culture will be worthless if a new hire joins the team who is not a successful fit.*

- *A good onboarding process gets the right people, who've been hired into the right seats, doing the right things the right way.*

- *Activating and amplifying the pride in new hires will help you build a better culture and reduce attrition.*

CHAPTER 4

The Cost of Inadequate Onboarding

The Retention Cost

Why do employees leave a company?

According to Leigh Branham, 89 percent of managers say people leave because they want more money. Yet when he analysed over 20,000 exit interviews with employees about why they really leave a company, 88 percent of employees will say it's not money, but other reasons, as shown in Figure 4.1 from Leigh's book, *The 7 Hidden Reasons Employees Leave: How to Recognise the Subtle Signs and Act Before It's Too Late.*

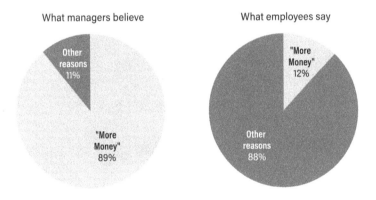

Figure 4.1 **What managers believe about reasons employees leave and why employees actually leave**

In the book, Branham identified the seven hidden reasons people leave as:

1 *The job or workplace was not as expected*

2 *The mismatch between job and person*

3 *Too little coaching and feedback*

4 *Too few growth and advancement opportunities*

5 *Feeling devalued and unrecognised*

6 *Stress from overwork and work-life balance*

7 *Loss of trust and confidence in senior leaders*

An effective 90-day onboarding process can significantly impact or overcome almost every one of these. We will discuss how to do this in the coming chapters.

And this connection is validated in my research, as shown in Figure 4.2, where 77 percent of respondents agreed that their onboarding process affects their attrition rate, defined as the number of people who leave their organisation each year.

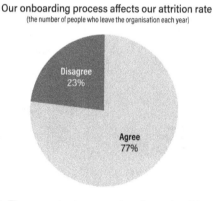

Our onboarding process affects our attrition rate
(the number of people who leave the organisation each year)

Figure 4.2 **The connection between onboarding and attrition rate**

You probably don't consider the fast-food industry when you think about how onboarding might affect your retention rate. Yet the fast-food restaurant Pal's Sudden Service from Kingsport, Tennessee, has seen only seven general managers resign in the past thirty-three years. Furthermore, only four unit managers have voluntarily left Pal's since 1981. Also, the annual turnover for assistant managers is 1.4 percent[9]. That's world-class retention in any

---

9 https://hbr.org/2016/01/how-one-fast-food-chain-keeps-its-turnover-rates-absurdly-low

industry, let alone the quick-service restaurant industry, where the overall turnover rate is about 73 percent[10].

Beyond this remarkable retention rate, there are other elements to Pal's business that are world-class. For example, service time is the first and most important metric in a drive-through fast-food restaurant. Service time is measured from when a car stops at the window until it begins driving off, and Pal's manages it within eighteen seconds. That's four times faster than the second-fastest quick-serve restaurant in the USA.

The second metric of importance is the error rate, and Pal's makes a mistake only once in every 3,600 orders, which is ten times better than the industry average. Pal's has managed to achieve the clear first position in retention and operational excellence by developing a comprehensive onboarding process that helps new hires deeply understand their role. According to Pal's President and CEO Thom Crosby, "Pal's is first and foremost a manufacturer. Our second job is to educate." And for employees, that education consists of hourly employees undertaking 120 hours of training and learning up to three positions, and managers are required to undertake eight hundred training hours.

It's likely the first name you often think of from the fast-food industry is McDonald's, and perhaps you consider that McDonald's has been very successful with only a fraction of Pal's onboarding hours for team members. And this is true, but McDonald's is a franchise, solving this retention and onboarding problem through different means. McDonald's has optimised their systems to accommodate high employee turnover, with systems that train employees to do a good job and then leave in less than a year.

But for leadership, McDonald's solves the retention problem by ensuring the store manager is also the franchise owner and being very selective in granting franchises. McDonald's accepts only around 1 percent of applicants to become franchisees. If accepted, they are required to complete a comprehensive training program that can take between nine and

10   https://www.dailypay.com/blog/qsr-and-restaurant-turnover-rates/

twenty-four months[11]. The training program is undertaken in part at individual McDonald's restaurants, online, and at the McDonald's Hamburger University campus in Oak Brook, Illinois. The program focuses on five key pillars — People, Operational Excellence, Sales and Marketing, Financial Growth, and Trust — ensuring that every franchise aligns with the whole system working towards a common goal[12].

You can be confident that these two industry-leading examples wouldn't spend this much time and money on new hires without a tangible return. And the first measure we should consider when evaluating the cost of inadequate onboarding is the attrition rate or the rate at which employees leave the firm. Within my research, I identified that the more likely a person is to agree with the statement "*after onboarding, new hires understand most of our company culture,*" the more likely they are to agree that their onboarding process affects their attrition rate. See Figure 4.3.

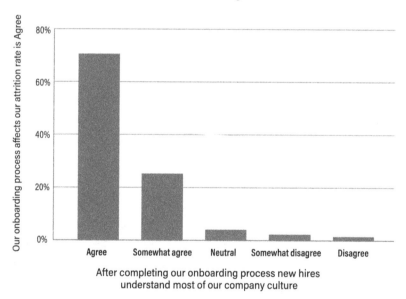

Figure 4.3 **The connection between an onboarding process and attrition rate**

---

11 https://smallbusiness.chron.com/need-open-mcdonalds-10513.html

12 https://www.mcdonalds.com/gb/en-gb/franchising/your-application/training.html

"Hold on just a second," one might say. "If we're going to exit new hires who are deemed an unsuccessful fit after 90 days, wouldn't that negatively impact the attrition rate?" Yes, exiting new hires who aren't a successful fit will impact the attrition rate. Still, during the first 90 days, if you are aware that the person isn't a successful fit, you can bet that other team members also know this and that even the new hire is probably thinking that this new job might not be ideal. There's even a good chance that the new hire is considering other options.

Employee engagement firm Tiny Pulse has identified that employees who rate their manager's performance poorly are four times more likely to be interviewing elsewhere[13]. Therefore, a manager's performance during the onboarding period becomes a critical factor affecting the first year's attrition rate. In addition, whether a person resigns or is fired, their direct manager is a crucial part of either decision.

Remember, people join companies and leave managers.

From an employer's perspective, the race is on once the new hire starts. There are 90 days to force a decision, whether it's a "hell yes!" or a "hell no!" on retaining the new hire before it's likely the legal circumstances of the situation change (see Chapter One for the specifics on this). If you can't define a new hire as a successful fit within 90 days, and you subsequently don't exit them for being an unsuccessful fit, they're probably going to stick around until they can find a better job elsewhere. That decision, a "hell yes!" or a "hell no!" is the job of the new hire's manager.

Across all employee turnover, about 20 percent is recorded within the first 90 days[14]. This concentration of employee turnover means that for every five people who sign an employment contract, join a company, and become a potential fit, only four will remain in 90 days. Once 18 months have

---

13 https://www.tinypulse.com/hubfs/2018%20Employee%20Retention%20Report.pdf

14 https://www.gnapartners.com/resources/articles/
why-an-employees-first-90-days-are-make-or-break]]

passed, around 46 percent of newly-hired employees have failed[15], having been pushed out, fired, or having quit. And for all the extra time and money spent to recruit leaders and executives, the results aren't much better, with 40 percent having left within 18 months[16].

In a separate survey[17], 90 percent of respondents said that the retention of new hires is an issue in their organisation. Nearly all (98 percent) said that onboarding programs are a key factor in retention efforts, and 69 percent have a formal onboarding program for all employees. However, very few programs last long enough to have any meaningful impact, with 53 percent saying their programs last seven days or less. For comparison, 49 percent of my survey respondents had an onboarding process of seven days or less. These turnover problems should not come as a surprise, given what we know about the impact of onboarding and just how rare great onboarding programs are.

Having established that onboarding and employee turnover are connected, we should consider the cost of turnover to a firm in hard dollar costs. From here, we can appreciate why companies like Pals or McDonald's would spend so much money and effort to minimise employee turnover, especially during the first 90 days. Also, we can build a case of why managers should spend time onboarding new hires and why we should spend money investing in onboarding programs.

When someone considers the cost of hiring an employee, they probably first think about the cost of an advert on a job board or a recruiter, and maybe the time for people in the Human Resources department to interview a candidate. So perhaps five or ten or twenty thousand dollars could be considered a reasonable cost to hire a person.

Why is it then that a manager will groan (and often swear) when someone

---

15 https://www.leadershipiq.com/blogs/
leadershipiq/35354241-why-new-hires-fail-emotional-intelligence-vs-skills

16 "Rise of a Headhunter" Brooke Masters, Financial Times, March 30, 2009

17 https://web.archive.org/web/20170507110156/http://www.kornferry.com/press/
korn-ferry-futurestep-survey-90-percent-of-executives-say-new-hire-retention-an-issue/

resigns? Or why wouldn't a manager exit a new hire who isn't a successful fit, knowing they will need to rehire if they exit them? These managers see the cost in time, effort, and productivity required to get another person into the role, fully understanding the culture, manager's expectations, and technical and process expectations.

Therefore, we must consider the cost of hiring in two different areas: firstly, the cost within the HR department, and then the much higher cost outside the HR department, as shown in Table 4.1.

Event	HR Department cost	Outside HR department cost
Employee departs	Exit interview	Meeting with manager
		Handover of work to a manager, understanding status of work in detail
		Final pay processing in admin
		Team covering the exited team member's workload, reducing their own productivity, or requiring overtime
		Reduced revenue if exited team member is in a sales role
		Severance cost
Hiring	Advertising costs	
	Recruiter costs	
	Interview time	Interview time with potential manager
	Offer negotiation	
Employee starts	Administration	On the job training
		Manager guiding and supervising
		Co-workers answering questions, lowering their productivity
		New hire's productivity takes 1-9 months to reach their predecessor
		Cost to maintain quality or rework as new hire learns

Table 4.1 **The cost of hiring inside and outside HR**

Recruiting, hiring, and training costs within an HR department can be relatively easy to calculate. For example, in Table 4.1, we could quickly estimate fifty hours in HR time plus advertising costs and recruiter costs where applicable. But what about the costs outside HR? Unless you have a financial analyst on hand, it would be difficult to measure something like the productivity decrease in co-workers or the direct time and opportunity cost of a manager during this event.

For a simple tool, let's look at Table 4.2 from *Forbes*[18], which should give you an off-the-shelf, ballpark estimate of the total hiring cost. If you're looking for a more accurate number, you can search online for the well-known Bliss-Gately spreadsheet.

Role	Cost of a hire
Entry-level / junior roles	50% of annual salary
Mid-level individual contributors	100% of annual salary
Mid-level managers	100% of annual salary
Senior-level individual contributors	125% of annual salary
Senior-level managers	125% of annual salary
Executives	200% of annual salary

Table 4.2 **The cost of hiring**

Now that we've considered the cost to hire, we can think about how often we need to hire. The average annual turnover rate for Australia and New Zealand was 17 percent in 2019[19], which is typical for most modern economies. You can calculate your turnover rate using the following formula. Simply divide the total number of leavers in a year by your average number of employees in a year. Then, multiply the total by one hundred. The number left is your annual staff turnover as a percentage.

For example, let's consider ACME manufacturing, a $30 million fictional company with one hundred employees. Acme had one hundred employees at the beginning of January and one hundred at the end of December. So, the average was one hundred. They had seventeen people leave during the year whose positions they had to rehire. Seventeen leavers divided by the

---

18 https://www.forbes.com/sites/billconerly/2018/08/12/
companies-need-to-know-the-dollar-cost-of-employee-turnover/#119de5aad590

19 https://www.ahri.com.au/media/4131/hr-industry-benchmark-survey-2019-standard-report.pdf

one hundred average equals 0.17. Multiply this by one hundred to get the 17 percent turnover rate for ACME manufacturing.

Table 4.3 looks at the breakdown of the seventeen leavers across ACME manufacturing and then applies the hire cost to these seventeen people.

Role	Number of hires in the past year (a)	Average salary (b)	Hire cost (c)	Total cost = a x b x c
Entry level / junior roles	7	$35,000	50% of annual salary	$122,500
Mid-level individual contributors	3	$65,000	100% of annual salary	$195,000
Mid-level managers	2	$70,000	100% of annual salary	$140,000
Senior-level individual contributors	1	$90,000	125% of annual salary	$112,500
Senior-level managers	2	$100,000	125% of annual salary	$250,000
Executives	1	$150,000	200% of annual salary	$300,000
	17		Total Cost	$1,120,000

Table 4.3 **Total cost of hiring example**

This hypothetical firm spent $1.12 million hiring people in the past year. Before any growth-related hiring, this was in line with the international average. Moreover, with only 1.4 resignations per month, the HR department probably believed they were doing well.

According to Glassdoor, 69 percent of employees stay at least three years if they have had a good onboarding experience[20]. Glassdoor further found that organisations with an effective onboarding process improve new hire retention by 82 percent and productivity by over 70 percent in the first year[21].

Let's go back to our fictional example ACME. You might remember this statistic from earlier in this chapter. "Once eighteen months have passed, around 46 percent of newly-hired employees have failed". So, what would happen if ACME could halve its attrition rate from seventeen to eight people

20 https://karesources.com/onboarding-done-right/

21 https://b2b-assets.glassdoor.com/the-true-cost-of-a-bad-hire.pdf

leaving within a year because of their onboarding efforts? Now, this isn't impossible; remember, Pal's Sudden Service has a 1.4 percent attrition for assistant managers against the industry average for all workers of 74 percent!

In Table 4.4, we see an example of the hiring cost if ACME halved its attrition rate.

Role	Number of hires in the past year. (a)	Average salary (b)	Hire cost (c)	Total cost = a x b x c
Entry level / junior roles	4	$35,000	50% of annual salary	$70,000
Mid-level individual contributors	1	$65,000	100% of annual salary	$65,000
Mid-level managers	1	$70,000	100% of annual salary	$70,000
Senior-level individual contributors	1	$90,000	125% of annual salary	$112,500
Senior-level managers	1	$100,000	125% of annual salary	$125,000
Executives	0	$150,000	200% of annual salary	$0
	8		Total Cost	$442,500

Table 4.4 Example of the impact of reduced attrition on the total cost of hiring

There's no doubt that I've used a hypothetical example to obtain a $677,500 saving, and the figures are for an example only. But even if we only look at the total hiring cost of $1.12 million and halve that, we have saved $560,000. And ACME manufacturing, with a ten percent profit, would need to sell an additional $5.6 million in goods to recapture that $560,000 in another form.

There is a real connection between your onboarding process and the attrition rate of your business. And that attrition comes at a cost that you can calculate and measure. So, let's now investigate how and why onboarding affects productivity and top performers.

The Cost to Productivity and Top Performers

Earlier in this chapter, I highlighted the statistic from Glassdoor that organisations with an effective onboarding process improve productivity by over 70 percent in the first year. Imagine if your car could legally reach your destination 70 percent faster, or you could personally earn 70 percent more per year!

Chapter 2 outlined how onboarding debt accrues when new hires don't understand the culture, managers' expectations, and technical and process expectations. As an example, if a recent hire understands only 50 percent of these three expectations after 90 days, then three things will occur:

- *They will take longer to become fully productive in their role*

- *They will be less productive during the time until they are fully productive in their role*

- *Once they become fully productive in their role, their productivity will be lower than what it potentially could be*

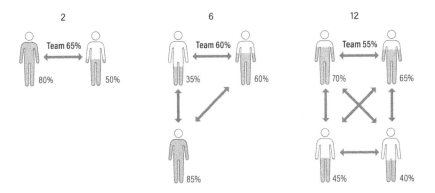

Figure 4.4 **Team onboarding debt as a team grows.**

In Figure 4.4, which shows team onboarding debt from Chapter 2, onboarding debt is carried in both individuals and teams, demonstrating why onboarding debt impacts both team and individual productivity.

The higher the onboarding debt, the higher the cost to productivity.

Imagine that a new hire completes their onboarding and is rated to understand an average of only 10 percent of the culture, the technical and process expectations, and the leader's expectations. Then another new hire is rated to have a 90 percent understanding of the same three things.

Indeed, the second new hire will be more productive, but without engaging a team of financial analysts, how can we understand the potential productivity cost in a simple manner?

In Chapter 2, I discussed the rating of a new hire to understand the onboarding debt they carry. In addition, I provided a sample score from a manager, as shown below.

- *Managers expectations – 6*

- *Cultural understanding – 6*

- *Technical/process understanding – 7*

Therefore, after 90 days, the new hire would average 67 percent understanding and be rated as carrying 33 percent onboarding debt. We can't directly say that is their productivity, but their understanding is certainly a strong indicator of their effectiveness.

During interviews with the most effective hiring managers and CEOs for this book, I learned that managers who had an effective 90-day onboarding process were confident that their new hires were more productive, faster. People told me their onboarding process had candidates fully productive in half the time they previously would. They told me that before building an effective onboarding process, it might have taken new hires six or nine months to be fully productive. They were now achieving the same thing in three months or less.

This increased productivity and speed to productivity was such an important, recurring theme from people I interviewed with effective onboarding processes that it became the subtitle of this book: *how to bring new hires to the point where they are more effective, faster.*

We can then consider Figure 4.5 to visualise the impact of an effective onboarding on productivity. At the 90-day mark, the new hires experiencing a below-average onboarding process are only about 35 percent productive, and those with an average onboarding are about 50 percent productive. In comparison, those encountering an effective onboarding process are around 90 percent productive. Only at the nine-month mark does the productivity between new hires begin to even out.

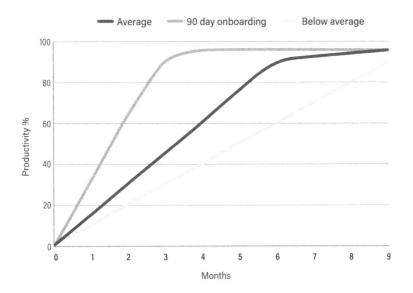

Figure 4.5 **Productivity impact by onboarding process quality**

What cost can we attribute to this difference in productivity that is meaningful and useful without the cost and time of a comprehensive financial analyst?

Let's compare the firms taking nine months to full productivity that we rated as "below average" to the 90-day onboarding process taking three months. The difference between the two in the overall quantity of productivity during those nine months is 40 percent lower.

Productivity is measured by dividing a firm's gross profit (revenue minus cost of goods sold) by the labour cost in a metric known as "Labour Efficiency Ratio," or LER. This metric for productivity comes from the book *Simple Numbers, Straight Talk, Big Profits!: 4 Keys to Unlock Your Business Potential* by Greg Crabtree. Put simply, this metric tells us how many dollars of gross profit we make for every dollar we pay to employees.

Across a firm, like in our ACME example, some people within the sales team might produce an LER as high as $6 or $8, whereas a pure administration person might not "produce" any gross profit directly at all and have an LER of $0. Yet across the entire firm, ACME has a Labour Efficiency Ratio of $2, meaning that for every dollar paid in wages, the firm achieves $2 in gross profit.

Looking at Table 4.5, we can see the same hires that ACME appointed that year. This table assumes that ACME has a "below-average" onboarding process, creating a 40 percent cost via poor productivity in the first nine months. This lost productivity is calculated using 75 percent of their annual productivity (nine months) multiplied by 0.4 (the productivity cost of 40 percent above).

Role	Number of hires in the past year (a)	Average salary (b)	Average productivity = b x $2 LER (c)	Lost productivity cost = c x 0.4 x 0.75 (d)	Total cost = a x d
Entry level / junior roles	7	$35,000	$70,000	$21,000	$147,000
Mid-level individual contributors	3	$65,000	$130,000	$39,000	$117,000
Mid-level managers	2	$70,000	$140,000	$42,000	$84,000
Senior-level individual contributors	1	$90,000	$180,000	$54,000	$54,500
Senior-level managers	2	$100,000	$200,000	$60,000	$120,000
Executives	1	$150,000	$300,000	$90,000	$90,000
	17			Total Cost	$648,000

Table 4.5 **Productivity cost example for new hires in the first year**

Note that ACME replaced people who left and did not grow the total number of team members across the year. So, the total productivity of the leavers, if they hadn't left, would have been $2,040,000, and this overall potential productivity was reduced by 32 percent or $648,000 because the "below average" onboarding process took nine months to get the new hires to full productivity rather than three months. While it's not the 70 percent productivity gain quoted by Glassdoor, it's an effective tool you can use to understand the productivity cost an ineffective onboarding might be costing you.

The dollar cost of an inadequate onboarding process for ACME includes $442,500 saved due to the attrition rate, plus $648,000 in productivity by decreasing the ascent to full productivity from nine months to three months. Therefore, a total of $1,090,500 could theoretically be saved in this business with $30m revenue by having managers responsible for new hires onboard eight new hires with an effective onboarding process.

Yet there is one more aspect to consider: the cost to top performers.

In Chapter 2, I attributed the phrase "we don't know why it didn't work" to a failed hire that people often call a "bad fit." We didn't follow a structured onboarding process, and the person has left.

Of course, the new hire probably has an opinion about why it didn't work.

They certainly didn't accept the job offer with the intent of leaving soon after. On the contrary, they were excited by reading your website's "About Us" page, where you had photos of laughing team members and information about the exciting work you do and why your core values matter. They were excited about the opportunities they saw in the job advert and what they learned at the job interview.

They signed the contract and were excited about their first day at the new job.

Then something happened.

At first, one or two things seemed a little strange. Then something didn't feel right, and next, they began to regret their decision. Eventually, they discovered a chasm between what they were promised and what the job, team, work, or boss turned out to be.

Their mind turned back to the job search. What other jobs are still available? What new jobs are available?

And they were determined to leave as soon as possible.

Of course, when they leave, most managers simply write it off as a bad fit.

This journey may seem unlikely in your experience, but the brutal reality is that about 30 percent[22] of job seekers have left a job within the first 90 days. The two most common reasons for leaving were company culture and the day-to-day job not meeting expectations.

"But they were a bad fit!" The exasperated manager might say. "They self-selected and saved me the effort of getting rid of them in the end!"

Remember, fit is not binary; fit is a spectrum. So perhaps they were, in fact, A players but felt the 1, or 7, or 14-day onboarding you currently provide wasn't representative of their expectations.

In Brad Smart's book *Topgrading (How to Hire, Coach and Keep A Players)*, he defines an A player as a person in the top ten percent of candidates at the pay rate you provide. They aren't getting paid more. They are simply the best.

Brad Smart states that the simple fact is that A players won't stay A players in a B player environment. Instead, they will either leave the company or drop to the B player level. Maybe some of the people who have been written off as a "bad fit" because they left could have been A players, but you provided a B player environment. Then they left to find an A player environment.

The question then becomes, who is more likely to quit in the first 90 days, a high performer with a trail of success who doesn't tolerate anything but the best in their career, or perhaps a mediocre, poor performer with a patchy history who only wants a job? According to Topgrading, A players only want

---

22 https://peakon.com/resources/library/the-four-phases-of-employee-experience/

to work in A player teams. So perhaps you're using a top-quality hiring process like Topgrading, which is producing A players who join your company. Then, if your onboarding process isn't at the A player standard, it might just repel those A players, who have many other options, and simply can't operate in an environment that isn't up to their standards.

I strongly recommend that you use an excellent hiring process like Topgrading. This is an essential step. But this book isn't about hiring. I've intentionally left that to other experts.

If you're going to the trouble of hiring A players, there is a risk they will leave if the culture or day-to-day job is not what they expect when they join. And team members know that there's a price to be paid when you hire great people and your onboarding process fails to integrate them into the business.

That's what my survey found, with Figure 4.6 demonstrating that 61 percent of respondents agreed they had hired great people, and their onboarding process failed to integrate them into the business well. Interestingly, the people who disagreed that their onboarding process had been unable to integrate the great people well were sixteen times more likely to disagree that their onboarding process affects their attrition rate. The reason, of course, is that many of them already had an effective onboarding process!

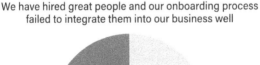

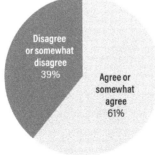

Figure 4.6 **Responses to question about great people who have been hired and not integrated into the business well**

Either your onboarding process successfully exits the people who aren't a fit, or without an effective onboarding process, you risk the top performers leaving and the poor performers remaining. And that is a separate, significant cost all its own.

In this chapter, we have considered the cost of inadequate onboarding on employee turnover, the productivity cost, and the cost to top performers.

Yet there is one critical cost within onboarding that we have not considered – the cost of forgetting.

The Cost of Forgetting

In the late 19th century, German psychologist Hermann Ebbinghaus tested his memory over a series of studies to understand how people remember information and how the mind loses information over time. The graph he plotted is represented in Figure 4.7, and it demonstrates how information disappears exponentially once we learn something.

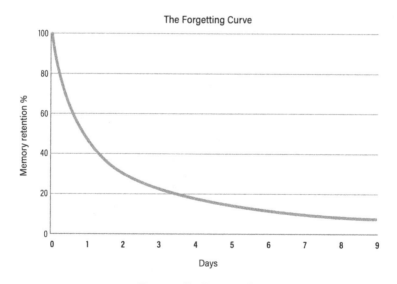

Figure 4.7 **The Forgetting Curve**

One day after learning new information, our retention drops to around 55 percent. However, by the time a week has passed, retention plummets to about 10 percent.

This incredible discovery is known as Ebbinghaus's Forgetting Curve and is the primary reason most onboarding processes are ineffective.

You may remember the data from Chapter 1, where my survey identified that 83 percent of recent hires undergo an onboarding process of 14 days or less. Furthermore, 49 percent of respondents had an onboarding process of seven days or less.

Inadequate onboarding is born of human nature and multiplied by human biology.

Human nature often leads managers to provide the minimum onboarding time, teaching essential items only once. Human biology means that new hires will likely forget 90 percent of what they are taught within a week.

One person I interviewed who shall remain nameless said, "I instruct new hires when they begin how 'I'm only going to tell you this once' and I onboard them in about one hour, and I explain if they don't remember what I tell them the first time, then they aren't good enough for the job."

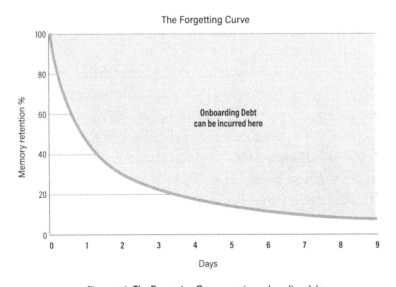

Figure 4.8 **The Forgetting Curve creating onboarding debt**

What if the new hire forgets 90 percent of the information after one week? We can then consider the forgotten things to form a part of onboarding debt, as illustrated in Figure 4.8.

However, not all is lost because subsequent research found that when we re-teach a concept, people remember it once again. For example, the first time information is re-taught, people once again forget 90 percent within a week. But that forgetting will be different from the initial rate of forgetting, as shown in Figure 4.9. When that information is taught a third time, something remarkable happens in the brain, and instead of forgetting 90 percent, a person forgets only 50 percent. Finally, when taught a fourth time, a person will retain 90 percent of the information taught!

And that's a concept that Matt Kuttler, CEO of Restockit.com, an online retailer of office, restaurant, and janitorial products, would do to onboard new hires. He would meet with new hires on their first day to discuss the company history, core values, and core purpose. He would then meet them again on their second week and revisit the history, core values, and core purpose with different stories explaining further and expanding on the first week's discussion. Then, on the fourth week, Matt would meet new hires and go over the same items again, reminding them through different stories while showing care for their progress and activating their pride. To an outsider, it might seem that Matt was repeating himself, but he was simply overcoming the forgetting curve.

And so, in the first month when a new hire joins the firm, the job of the new hire's manager becomes clearer. They need to use the first month to overcome the forgetting curve through a series of meetings with new hires. Before the new hire transitions to their second month of onboarding, the objective is to recall at a basic level of understanding the culture, the technical and process expectations, and their manager's expectations. We can achieve this through a series of weekly meetings, each improving memory retention, as shown in Figure 4.9.

Overcoming this forgetting curve is why I called the first 30 days the "understand" stage, as shown in Figure 4.10. Managers need to overcome the forgetting curve during this stage and be confident that new hires can

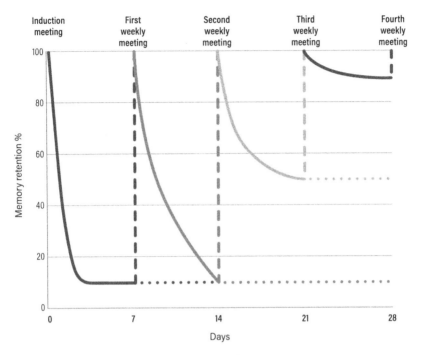

Figure 4.9 Overcoming the forgetting curve

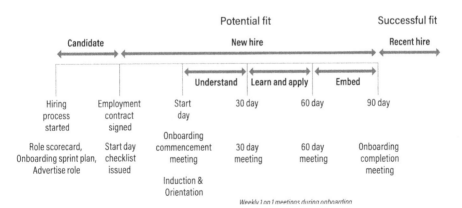

Figure 4.10 Onboarding process terminology

understand. However, this doesn't mean repeating the same thing for four weeks in a row. For example, you could tell a different core values story for each of your core values each week. In this way, you reinforce the same core values from different perspectives.

This cost of forgetting, leading to onboarding debt, the cost of productivity, and the cost of retention all add up to significant amounts very quickly, as shown. Every firm pays a tangible cost for the quality of their onboarding process, and the costs compound. You might understand how to hire the right people in the right seats, but without an effective onboarding process, you might not understand just how to have those people do the right things in the right way.

An effective hiring process gets the right people in the right seats.

An effective onboarding process validates that they are, in fact, the right people and gets them doing the right things the right way. But to achieve that, an effective onboarding process must also filter out those who are an unsuccessful fit.

And filtering out those who are an unsuccessful fit might mean short-term pain.

In the next chapter, we will discuss the short-term pain of acting on the unsuccessful fit versus the long-term gain.

Key Points

- *An ineffective onboarding process will negatively impact a firm's attrition rate, and every additional hire required might cost 100 percent of their salary*

- *Organisations with an effective onboarding process improve productivity up to 70 percent in the first year*

- *The higher the onboarding debt, the higher the cost to productivity*

- *An ineffective onboarding process can inadvertently cause top performers (A players) to leave and mediocre performers to stay*

- *People forget 90 percent of what they learn within seven days but can retain over 90 percent if they are re-taught several times*

- *Every firm pays a tangible cost for the quality of their onboarding process and the costs compound*

CHAPTER 5

Short Term Pain Versus Long Term Gain

The Real Problem with Onboarding

Why is inadequate onboarding so common?

In the previous chapter, I mentioned how "only" 12 percent of employees strongly agree that their organisation does a great job onboarding new staff. Having now reviewed the impact that both a good and bad onboarding has on a company over the previous chapters of this book, how is it possible that it has such an enormous impact, and yet so few firms do a great job of it?

Onboarding is a "once in a while" process without a clear owner.

You're probably very clear about who is accountable for sales at your firm. You're probably clear on who is accountable for ordering supplies and who pays the supplier invoices. And you're clear about who is accountable for resolving computer issues. And by accountable, I mean if they consistently do an inadequate job, they will probably be fired.

Depending on your firm's size, all those things could be full-time roles, and perhaps they are the full-time focus within those roles. In addition, there might be supporting tasks or processes that lead to completing those tasks, but they are in silos and sit within a specific department or process.

Perhaps you even know who is accountable for hiring. Maybe it's managers, Human Resources, or your People and Culture department.

But hiring has a very clear outcome: to fill a role. If the position is filled, the job is done. People then move on and get back to work. Sure, it's a part-time distraction from a person's day-to-day role, but there is a clear success metric. Vacancy filled.

Let's move on and get back to work.

But, as shown in Figure 5.1, onboarding is perhaps the only key process that needs to be performed by the entire organisation which doesn't have a clear owner. According to Allied Workforce, even before we consider clear ownership, management participates in onboarding programs at only

35 percent of companies[23].

Onboarding doesn't have a clear outcome like "vacancy filled" does for hiring. If someone does an inadequate job of onboarding, there's likely no chance they will be fired. Onboarding doesn't contribute to a clear objective in the way other processes do, where that objective might directly lead to more sales or faster project completion.

And onboarding is part-time. A busy manager might only perform an onboarding process once every three or six months.

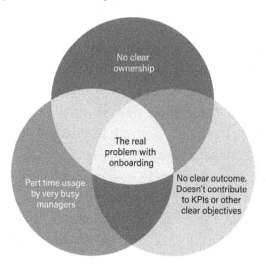

Figure 5.1 **The real problem with onboarding**

We now know the qualitative and quantitative costs to the firm, as detailed in the previous chapters. Also, we learned that inadequate onboarding has a significant impact on the new hire's manager. And managers are undoubtedly aware of that, with 92% of my survey respondents agreeing with the statement, *"If recent hires who report to me understood my expectations within 90 days, my job would be easier."*

In my book *Made to Thrive: The Five Roles to Evolve Beyond Your Leadership Comfort Zone*, I explained how leaders or CEOs have five roles, one of which

23 https://learn.g2.com/onboarding-statistics

is "to create a positive culture that unites the team and attracts the right people." Looking at Figure 5.2, we can see the CEO performing this role on the right. On the left, the hiring manager is responsible for signing new hires who are a potential fit. It's simply impossible to sign new hires who are a successful fit; what we get from a hiring manager is a potential fit. We find out whether a new hire, that potential fit, is a successful or an unsuccessful fit during the onboarding process.

Onboarding, when considered through the lens of culture, is a bridge between the role of the hiring process, often owned by a hiring manager, and the cultural role of the CEO, as shown in Figure 5.2. Notably, the hiring manager and the CEO have very different outcomes related to culture.

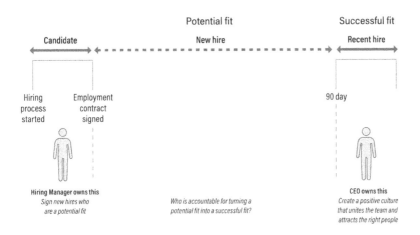

Figure 5.2 **Hiring managers and CEOs have different roles in culture**

The hiring manager seeks to sign new hires aligned with the culture who are a potential fit.

The CEO seeks to create a positive culture that unites the team and attracts the right people.

The role of onboarding is to connect these two goals by integrating a successful fit with the culture or exiting an unsuccessful fit. This way, as demonstrated in Figure 5.3, onboarding could be viewed as a bridge between the hiring process and the ongoing culture process.

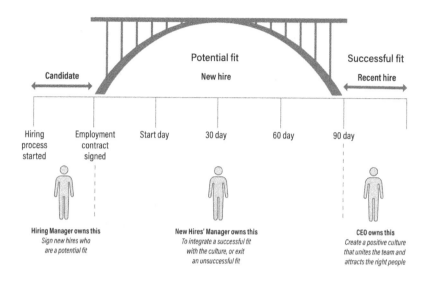

Figure 5.3 **Onboarding is the bridge between the hiring manager and the CEO**

As challenging as it is, the new hire's manager must own the onboarding process for that new hire. An onboarding process will fail if it is owned by HR or People and Culture. An HR or People and Culture department must support onboarding, but they can't own onboarding. Equally, if onboarding is something that HR must harass or nag a manager to complete so they can complete their own form or checklist, it will fail.

And there must be a complete buy-in from the CEO and executives of the organisation. As Josh Gardner, one of the leaders I interviewed, put it, "Everyone must have a sense of ownership; if the executives don't do it, people will feel cynical and won't invest in it."

How can we overcome this lack of ownership and accountability?

One way is to encourage teams to think about an investment in hiring as a two-part process.

First, a firm commits to no more than the hiring and onboarding costs. A leader will allocate funds to hire and onboard a new hire for the first 90 days only.

Second, after evidence from the new hire's manager that they are a successful fit, funding can be approved by the hiring manager's manager for a full-time salary. Again, this evidence needn't be overly cumbersome. It's just evidence that the hiring manager has completed their onboarding sprint plan, and a formal final meeting has been held. See the following chapters for information on the onboarding sprint plan and the final meeting.

The power of this approach is that it amplifies the importance of an evidence-based, successful or unsuccessful fit decision. It forces the manager to apply for a second round of "funding" being the ongoing salary of the new hire, using the evidence of the process. And it places compliance with the system solely on the new hire's manager.

Finally, it changes the outcome of an onboarding process, from new hire learning to new hire fit.

Only the new hire's manager can confidently say whether a person is a successful or unsuccessful fit.

And managers can gain that confidence by viewing the onboarding process as the last in a series of filters, starting with a group of candidates and ending with a successful fit.

The Last Filter

To safely deliver water to your home, water utilities take the water in your pipes through a series of treatment processes before it is safe to drink. In essence, these water treatment processes:

- *Filter large particles*

- *Filter sediment*

- *Filter sand, gravel, and charcoal*

- *Disinfect*

In hiring, we firstly place a job advert on a job board, engage a recruiter, and encourage a large pool of candidates to apply. We then filter those candidates down to a shortlist of people who may be qualified or suitable to perform the role. From that list, we filter down to another list of people with whom we might have a telephone interview, and then that list is further filtered down to a list that we will interview. Ideally, after we have filtered through all the candidates, we might end up with two or three suitable candidates to make a hiring decision. We would then decide and sign a contract.

Is that candidate then "safe to drink" for the firm using the water treatment metaphor?

No, the onboarding process is the last filter to prevent people from coming in and damaging the culture or the business. The managers and leaders are the custodians of the culture and are accountable for the business results. Letting in a toxic person or someone who doesn't fit in and can affect the team is the new hire's manager's responsibility. They own the last filter. But it must be an effective last filter with an engaged manager.

The shorter an onboarding process, the less likely a manager will know whether a poor onboarding has affected the team, as shown in Figure 5.4.

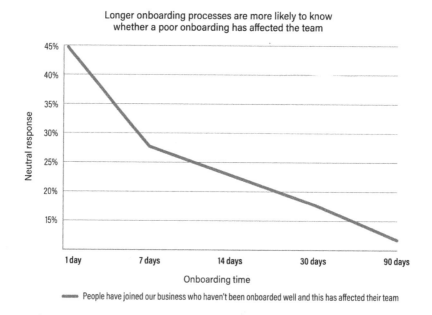

Figure 5.4 **Confidence in a longer onboarding process affecting a team**

Many people who experience a 1-or-7-day process and, to a lesser degree, a 14-day process, are not sure of the link between their onboarding and how it affects their team. Forty-five percent of respondents with a 1-day process neither agreed nor disagreed with the statement, "*People have joined our business who haven't been onboarded well, and this has affected their team.*"

New hires want their managers to be involved and show them the ropes. According to one LinkedIn study, 96 percent of over 14,000 respondents said the most important thing in a one-on-one interview is to get to know the supervisor[24]. In another LinkedIn study, 72 percent of employees said that one-on-one time with their direct manager is the most important part of the onboarding process[25].

In my survey, I asked respondents whether they agreed with the statement, "*My direct reports understand my expectations of them to the point it's not possible for them to misunderstand.*" Those who disagreed with that statement were then twenty-three times more likely to disagree with another statement, "*After completing our onboarding process, new hires understand most of their manager's expectations.*"

The only time that direct reports can truly learn their manager's expectations is during the onboarding process. And in fact, 56 percent of respondents in my survey agreed that 90 days after a new hire has started is too late to begin any new onboarding tasks.

Some new hires will not understand or perhaps not even want to understand their manager's expectations. Some will not understand or agree with the technical or process expectations. And some will feel like the culture is like fingernails scratching a chalkboard.

That's okay. The onboarding process aims to filter out those who are an unsuccessful fit.

And an onboarding process can only be successful if those deemed an unsuccessful fit exit.

---

24 https://karesources.com/onboarding-done-right/

25 https://enboarder.com/2018/11/01/
employee-onboarding-new-hire-retention-turnover-rates/

Success Means Exiting

"A point of view is worth 80 IQ points, but a change of perspective is worth another 80 IQ points."
ALAN KAY

Tim was dumbfounded. His face was blank, and he didn't know what to say. I'd just explained to him that the onboarding process he'd developed, presented to the leadership team, and was so proud of, would not work if it didn't plan to exit some new hires. Like so many leaders, Tim was confident that there is one decision, and that happens when we hire. Maybe he was thinking, "That's the deal done. We've signed the contract. Onboarding then helps people learn to perform better." It seemed entirely illogical to consider exiting new hires they'd spent so much time and effort trying to hire. To have someone exit after 90 days might have seemed a failure.

An exit is a success, not a failure, with an effective onboarding process.

For Josh Gardner, one of the executives I interviewed, the best onboarding process he had ever seen turned out terrible for him. Josh explains, "They did an incredible job of caring about the onboarding. I knew who I could turn to for any question. I knew who to turn to about the values and norms and who to talk to about expectations for the role and resources." The best onboarding process he'd seen was one where he ended up exiting as an unsuccessful fit. Josh still seemed grateful for the experience, and I sensed that he knew the strength of their process with hindsight meant that it probably wouldn't work out in the long term in any case.

In the book *Necessary Endings: The Employees, Businesses, and Relationships That All of Us Have to Give Up in Order to Move Forward*, Dr. Henry Cloud demonstrates that, when done well, "necessary endings" allow us to stop the pain, foster growth, reach personal and business goals, and live better lives. When done poorly, good opportunities are lost, and misery remains or is repeated. While we all face these kinds of endings daily, Dr. Cloud finds that most of us fall in the latter category and don't handle endings very well.

Sixty-two percent of people I surveyed agreed with the statement, "We have hired the wrong people, and our onboarding process failed to exit them as part of that process." Your onboarding process must exit the wrong people to be effective. If 100 percent of new hires pass your onboarding process and become a successful fit, perhaps your onboarding process isn't rigorous enough.

Or, put another way, if your hiring process gets it right 90 percent of the time, your onboarding process should aim to exit the remaining 10 percent. And no hiring process will ever get it right 100 percent of the time.

A recent study from Leadership IQ[26] found that 82 percent of hiring managers responsible for recently hired failures reported that, in hindsight, they saw subtle clues that the candidate would fail. Yet, they didn't act because they were too focused on other issues, pressed for time, or lacked confidence in their interviewing abilities.

When we don't invest time to onboard new hires well, we are gambling on the likelihood that a new hire will succeed. So, the short-term gain of saving time by spending as little time as possible with the new hire is traded against the long-term gain that the new hire will succeed or the gain they will exit if they're an unsuccessful fit.

Short-term gain equals long-term pain.
Short-term pain equals long-term gain.

Let's revisit the onboarding success matrix from Chapter 2 in Figure 5.5.

---

26 https://www.leadershipiq.com/blogs/
leadershipiq/35354241-why-new-hires-fail-emotional-intelligence-vs-skills

Figure 5.5 **Onboarding success matrix with fit definitions**

When we look to achieve a good fit, we make a trade-off every time we hire a person. A new hire's manager decides between spending more time upfront with the recent hire or more time later coaching, managing, and course-correcting things they don't understand.

To follow a process as I've outlined in this book, managers will produce either a successful or unsuccessful fit.

But the problem is that if the process is followed and it results in an unsuccessful fit, the manager needs to begin the entire hiring process again, creating more work for them.

So, the real challenge for a manager becomes, is it worth it?

Is it worse to be stuck with the new hire who can't handle the work and who is damaging to the team or to publicly admit that you've made a mistake?

Is it worth following this process which will take three months to onboard a new hire? Is it worth taking the extra time on something that used to take only a couple of hours? Is it worth the risk that you might discover they are an unsuccessful fit, which means you will have to rehire again?

In her book *Wilful Blindness: Why We Ignore the Obvious at Our Peril*, author Margaret Heffernan argues that the most significant threats and dangers we face are those we don't see – not because they're secret or invisible, but because we're willfully blind to them. As she states, "You cannot fix a problem that you refuse to acknowledge."

And managers can easily fall into this wilful blindness trap.

Managers worried about exiting an unsuccessful fit and starting the recruiting process again can become willfully blind to the fact that they now need to manage this person. As shown in Figure 5.6, the manager follows one of three paths. Either they have produced an unsuccessful fit and need to start recruiting again, or they have a successful fit and need to begin the ongoing management of the person. Or they don't want to know that they have an unsuccessful fit. Therefore, they need to start the ongoing management of the person.

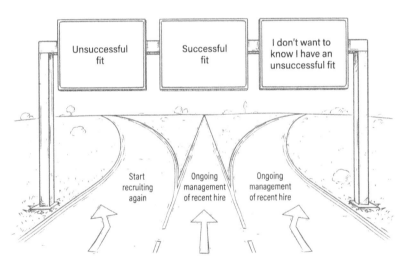

Figure 5.6 **Onboarding compliance challenge for manager**

If you find yourself in a situation where you need to exit a person, I encourage you to seek legal advice and/or expert professional assistance relevant to your situation. You must be confident that you comply with your company's and country's laws relating to employment law. This book is general in nature and is not intended to provide advice specific to your situation.

Should you find yourself doubting a new hire and wondering what to do, Matt Kuttler, CEO of Restockit.com, suggests managers go back and review the core values and job responsibilities of the role and then rank the new hire on a one-to-five scale against all of these. This simple assessment will give you a more quantifiable view of the situation when you might be unsure.

If you begin to feel that there is a risk a new hire might become an unsuccessful fit, you should act. First, use the weekly onboarding meeting to provide direct feedback and a status update. These meetings are designed to drive course correction and alignment with focused feedback. See the following two chapters for more on these meetings.

When providing corrective feedback, you should prepare for a direct and probably uncomfortable conversation with the new hire. And it would be best if you considered the cost to keep or exit the new hire, using the many examples provided in this book. But don't leave it till the last minute. A lot of clear coaching and feedback around identified outcomes offers the best chance of a successful fit. But if the new hire is not progressing well, they should know it.

The day you exit an unsuccessful fit should be no surprise to either party.

Long-term gain from onboarding occurs when managers prepare. And that is what we will discuss in the next chapter, Chapter 6: Preparing to Effectively Onboard.

Key Points

- *For many firms, onboarding has no clear ownership, no clear outcome, and is a part-time process.*

- *The only time that direct reports can truly learn their manager's expectations is during the onboarding process.*

- *An exit is a success, not a failure, with an effective onboarding process.*

- *The only time that direct reports can understand their expectations is during the onboarding process.*

- *If your hiring process gets it right 90 percent of the time, your onboarding process should aim to exit the remaining 10 percent.*

CHAPTER 6

Preparing to Effectively Onboard

The Role Scorecard

You might remember in Chapter 4 when I said, "An effective onboarding process validates that they are, in fact, the right people and gets them doing the right things the right way."

We can then consider this chapter preparing us to validate new hires and get them to do the right things the right way.

Like painting a house, onboarding creates most of the final success during the preparation period. But an effective onboarding process should not take up an excessive amount of a manager's time.

Let's look at an example of the complete time commitment for a manager who is onboarding a new hire. This example assumes four weeks in a month; adjust the time up and down relative to your situation.

Preparation – Role scorecard – 2 hours
Preparation – Onboarding sprint plan – 1 hour
The first day meet with a new hire – 2 hours
First month – 1 hour per week – 4 hours
Second month – 45 mins per week – 3 hours
Third month – 30 mins per week – 2 hours
Onboarding close meeting – 1 hour

Total – 15 hours

Say you're a manager on $100,000 per annum. Depending on how the week is structured, this might cost the firm around $650 per new hire in the manager's time spent onboarding. So, for example, $100,000 divided fifty-two weeks, divided by forty-five working hours, then multiplied by fifteen hours. Now I know that's not how it really works in a knowledge worker role. I know that much of the other work might still need doing. If you have a hectic schedule, the onboarding process may not be viewed as essential.

But what if the small amount of time you commit to this onboarding process made your job easier?

Building a role scorecard is an example of what Jim Collins, author of *Good to Great* and several other business classics, calls "clock building."

According to Jim's website jimcollins.com, "Clock Building is a concept developed in Jim's book *Built to Last*. Leading as a charismatic visionary — a 'genius with a thousand helpers' — is time telling; shaping a culture that can thrive far beyond any single leader is clock building. Searching for a single great idea on which to build success is time telling; building an organisation that can generate many great ideas over a long period of time is clock building. Enduring greatness requires clock building."

During a recent interview, Jim explained how every person writes a "bible" for their seat at his research firm in Boulder, Colorado.

As Jim says, "At our firm, every seat has the ten commandments of that seat. When a person in that seat leaves, the bible is there. Four times per year, each person in a seat needs to update and submit their bible on their seat for approval."

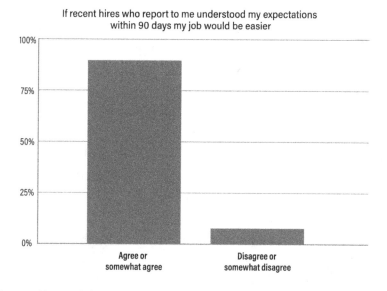

Figure 6.1 Managers believe their jobs will be easier if new hires understand their expectations

A role scorecard is not the same as Jim's "bible," but it's drawn from a similar principle. Once you build a role scorecard for a role, it should last. You're clock building, as Jim puts it. Then when you need to hire for that role again in the future, the role scorecard may require a slight review and modification, but it's there and ready to go. As a result, you've made it easier for new hires to understand your expectations.

And managers certainly know the importance of new hires understanding their expectations, as shown in Figure 6.1, with 92 percent of respondents agreeing that if recent hires understood their expectations within 90 days, their job would be easier.

In my book *Made to Thrive*, I outline how there are three criteria to assess any employee. They are Capable, Understand, and Want:

In developing the accountability side of your business, it's crucial that you ensure every employee understands exactly what is expected of them and what it takes for them to succeed in their role, to the point where it is not possible to misunderstand what they must do to succeed.

This is the uncomfortable truth that many leaders are reluctant to admit. When I work with leadership teams and determine the people who are not performing, we dig down and ask why the person in question isn't performing as expected by asking three key questions:

1 *Are they capable of succeeding in the role?*

2 *Do they understand what it takes to succeed in the role?*

3 *Do they want to succeed in the role?*

The reason it is an uncomfortable truth is that many times we identify that the employee actually doesn't understand what it takes to succeed in the role to the point where it is not possible to misunderstand. Of the three questions, this is the question that most speaks to the leader's effectiveness in setting the person up for success.

It is simply unfair for a leader to fail to empower employees to succeed by not giving them an understanding of how to succeed in the organisation.

And yet it is by far the greatest obstacle to building accountability. If people aren't completely clear on how to succeed, it is hypocritical to hold them accountable when they fail to succeed.

That's the key to building an effective role scorecard. First, it should make the manager completely clear how an employee will succeed after their onboarding. Then a separate document called the onboarding sprint plan, detailed later in this chapter, provides a map of how a new hire will get there.

A new hire might be capable of succeeding in their role, and they might want to succeed in the role. But whether they understand how to succeed in the role is the manager's responsibility through onboarding, and that understanding begins by building a role scorecard.

A manager uses the role scorecard in four separate areas.

1 *In hiring, it paints a clear picture of the type of person you are looking for to fill the role that you can compare against during the hiring process. You can rate each candidate against the criteria within the role scorecard.*

2 *During onboarding, you can clearly explain the expectations and set clear goals.*

3 *After onboarding and when the person has exited their probation, you can effectively measure their performance against a scorecard.*

4 *During performance management, you have a clear and specific document created before the person starts the role that you can use for robust discussions.*

A manager must build a role scorecard before advertising a vacancy or talking with candidates. The role scorecard will inform you how to write the job advert and provide tips to interview and rate candidates against the criteria set within the role scorecard. You can also share the role scorecard with candidates to clarify expectations during the hiring process. If you're in a larger organisation, the role scorecard's completion should probably be a minimum requirement before you are permitted to advertise a vacancy.

Managers should use role scorecards in two ways: to clarify the role and measure each candidate against the role's expectations.

Clarifying the role means understanding the main elements of a role, ensuring that you can assess candidates objectively against set criteria. Measuring each candidate means at the end of each interview, interviewers complete the role scorecard to assess the candidates' alignment with the pre-determined criteria after the candidate has left.

The five components of a role scorecard are:

1 *Role Purpose – Outlining in a sentence or two why the job exists and its purpose within the company.*

2 *Responsibilities – The functions, systems, and outputs the role is responsible for.*

3 *Specific measures of success – The results you want to go from A to B by a certain date. For example, sales from $1m to $1.5m by the end of 2024.*

4 *Competency expectations – A list of the must-have competencies across three criteria: the culture, managers' expectations, and technical and process expectations. For example, "analysis skills" would be a necessary technical competency for a CFO role, while "risk-taking" would not be required. After each interview, this is used to rate*

Role Scorecard example	
Position	Sales manager
Role purpose	Reporting to the CEO, the sales manager is accountable for effectively leading the sales team to achieve the firm's revenue and gross margin budget
Responsibilities	Lead the sales department in day-to-day people management and ensure team compliance in line with the overall company goals and needs. Hire, coach, train, and hold accountable sales team members to achieve their sales budget individually, thereby contributing to the overall budget. Develop credibility for the sales team function within the business by providing timely and accurate sales insights, analysis of sales trends, sales reports, and sales team trends to support the CEO and other senior executives in making the best decisions in line with company strategy. Be fully responsible for the firm's revenue and gross margin dollar results, including the negative impact of any discounting initiative. Work with the marketing manager to coordinate sales team efforts and maximise marketing spend. Manage all sales recruiting and performance management within the sales team. Regularly develop new initiatives for sales team training and sales team effectiveness on both sales techniques and our products for customers.
Specific measures of success	**Key measure of success:** Gross margin dollars sold per month to budget. Greater than $6m per month **Other measures** Revenue: > $15m per month by July 2023 Sales team performance: >80% always achieve individual budget Sales team retention: >80% retention per annum Sales pipeline: increase to $50m by October 2023
Competency expectations	**Cultural expectations:** The team expresses pride in working for the sales manager, will rally the sales team to achieve budget when behind, must have a legacy of sales management success, communicate transparently up and down, celebrate wins with the team, and set achievable goals. **Manager's expectations:** Relies on a CRM to achieve results, quick to build trust with team and customers, professional presentation every day, communicates immediately if a customer is thinking about cancelling a contract, any product issues should generate a leadership meeting within three days, and every salesperson follows the documented sales process. **Technical and process expectations:** Proficient in Salesforce, competent in managing out underperforming salespeople, managing customer delivery against manufacturing output, clearly interacting with customers about technical challenges our product solves, and training others on the Quality Assurance system related to the sales team.
Candidate summary	

Table 6.1 **Role Scorecard example**

the candidate's competency against the criteria. Cultural expectations within the role scorecard should be more specific to the role than the core values and behaviours described in Chapter 3.

5 *Candidate summary – A list of strengths, areas of concern, and recommendations about each candidate completed at the end of each interview.*

In Table 6.1, you can see an example role scorecard. You can also download an editable version of this and other tools with a further explanation at my website: evolutionpartners.com.au.

The role scorecard clearly outlines success when a person is effective in a role. However, an effective onboarding process passes through three distinct stages to reach that point. In the next section, we will look at the three stages of onboarding.

The Three Stages of Onboarding

Let's review the onboarding process terminology in Figure 6.2 and look at these three distinct stages.

- *We have the "understand" stage between the start day and the 30-day point.*

- *We have the "learn and apply" stage between the 30-day and 60-day points.*

- *We have the "embed" stage between the 60-day and 90-day points.*

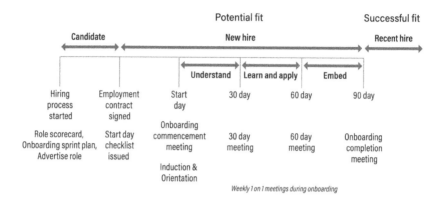

Figure 6.2 **Onboarding process terminology**

This segmentation is essential before considering your onboarding sprint plan and how we deal with new hires in each of the three distinct stages.

Let's take the example of a salesperson.

They may be attending sales meetings alongside other salespeople as observers in the understand stage.

In the learn and apply stage, they may be attending and running sales meetings, with another salesperson attending as an observer.

They may be attending sales meetings alone in the embed stage yet providing detailed updates to their manager after each meeting.

If a new salesperson has been in the role for 75 days and is still attending many sales meetings as an observer, there is very little chance that in fifteen days, on day 90, they will be able to manage sales calls alone. The salesperson in this example is still performing tasks from the understand stage. This is a red flag for their manager that they must take action.

Across the three onboarding stages, the manager of the new hire transitions through five distinct roles during onboarding.

Here are those five roles with some examples of each:

Directing – "The bathrooms are over there," "We use Salesforce as a CRM, and here are your login details."

Teaching – "With ACME manufacturing, we tend to get $1m of orders per month," "Ron plays golf every Friday."

Advising – "You should call Ron before lunch on Tuesday," "You should complete the CRM updates after each meeting."

Mentoring – "Make calls before lunch to solve that problem," "Call at least seven times to get the decision-maker."

Coaching – "What calls do you have this week, and where are you stuck?", "What can you do to identify the decision-maker?"

I'm not certain there is a specific way to navigate these transitions because every role and person is different. But I am certain that at the end of the onboarding process, you will likely need to traverse each of these, and your goal should be to have an established coaching relationship with the new hire as their manager. As a manager, you want team members to be accountable to the team goal and focus your time coaching them to achieve that goal.

Sometimes it's not easy transitioning through each of these stages to end up coaching. It's human nature to want to provide advice instead of coach direct reports. As Michael Bungay Stanier, author of *The Coaching Habit: Say Less, Ask More & Change the Way You Lead Forever* explains, "The advice monster believes you're better than the other person. To tame your advice monster, what you want to do is replace your advice-giving habit with a new habit: Staying curious."

Through the onboarding process, the agenda for meetings should transition from initially being about the manager and the company's what, how, and why into being mainly about the new hire, their issues, and their results. You'll find more about agendas in the next chapter.

When viewing these three stages of understand, learn and apply, and embed, consisting of around 30 days per each stage, remember that new hires need to unlearn many things they learned at their last job. It will take time to remove those old habits and unlearn how they previously did things. Onboarding debt is carried not only when new hires fail to understand but also when they fail to unlearn from their last role.

And it's onboarding debt that reduces in an S curve pattern, as shown in Figure 6.3. After 30 days, a new hire in an effective onboarding process has most likely overcome the forgetting curve and is likely recounting much of what they have learned. Moving into the learn and apply stage, the new hire uses the things they understood in the first 30 days and learns from their on-the-job experience. Finally, in the embed stage, the manager transitions to establishing more of a mentoring and coaching role.

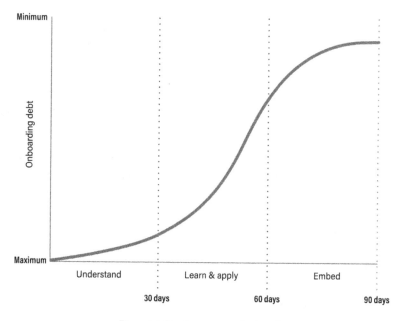

Figure 6.3 **The three stages of onboarding**

According to James Clear, it takes more than two months before a new behaviour becomes automatic — 66 days to be exact. And that is one other reason I'm advocating a 90-day onboarding process. Once we have completed the first two stages – understand and then learn and apply-- the new hire has formed the habits of success in the new role, and the habits have become automatic.

Here is an overview outlining the three stages of onboarding.

The first 30 days – Understand

The goal is to confidently exit the new hire from the understand stage and have them enter the learn and apply stage at the 30-day mark. Using a series of four weekly meetings, the manager should overcome the "forgetting curve." Ideally, through those weekly meetings, there should be a feeling from the new hire's manager that they have explained most of the stuff and that the purpose of the weekly onboarding meetings is beginning to feel a little pointless. If you get that feeling, you're on the right track! New hires should have completed all the items on the onboarding sprint plan detailed later in this chapter before moving out of the understand stage and into month two.

The second 30 days – Learn and apply

The goal of the learn and apply stage is to confidently exit the new hire from the learn and apply stage and have them enter the embed stage at the 60-day mark. Continuing the weekly meeting format, the manager should be transitioning from directing and teaching to advising and perhaps mentoring. The onboarding sprint plan will have fewer items for the new hire to complete in this stage compared to the first stage. The time during meetings is used to ask questions like, "What did you learn?" or "Where were you stuck when you did that?" New hires should have completed all the items on the onboarding sprint plan detailed later in this chapter before moving out of the embed stage into month three.

The third 30 days – Embed

The goal of the embed stage is to confidently classify the new hire as a successful fit at the 90-day meeting, which concludes the onboarding process.

If new hires stop the onboarding process at the 60-day mark, they may revert to their old habits. The embed stage embeds the new habits they have understood, learnt, and applied. Continuing the weekly meeting format, the manager should be transitioning from advising and mentoring to coaching.

The manager should easily transition from the final onboarding stages, where they coach the new hire, into an ongoing coaching process and meeting rhythm after the onboarding process is complete.

It can be easy to view a structured process of weekly meetings for three months as a difficult habit to maintain for busy managers, especially once a new hire begins producing results. But if viewed as a three-stage process, where the new hire is transitioning from being directed at the beginning to being coached at the end, it can be valuable. And that real value only comes when you develop and execute an onboarding sprint plan.

The Onboarding Sprint Plan

Every new hire at the Las Vegas online shoe retailer Zappos goes through the same training as the customer loyalty team reps, regardless of department or title. So, it wouldn't matter if you were a new accountant, lawyer, or software developer: you will still spend the first two weeks on the phone, in the call centre, helping customers with their online purchases. According to the late founder Tony Hsieh, this provides a valuable lesson about the culture at Zappos, how the processes work, and the types of issues that customers regularly have. Furthermore, it means that after their two weeks working in the call centre, new hires have developed a unique cohort of friends across the firm and can begin their regular job with a genuine sense of purpose.

Curating experiences like these can create an impactful impression on a new hire. In the book *The Power of Moments: Why Certain Experiences Have Extraordinary Impact*, authors Chip and Dan Heath demonstrate how, in our lives, there are certain moments or experiences that have a lasting, profound impact on people. For example, think about your experience at a wedding or moving into a new house. Or perhaps even a car accident. We can remember these moments and how these events made us feel with much greater clarity than everyday experiences around them.

Chip and Dan Heath ask, "Many of the defining moments in our lives are the result of accident or luck—but why would we leave our most meaningful, memorable moments to chance when we can create them?" As we begin to look at the onboarding sprint plan, we should remember that we also want to build memorable moments into the plan as we consider all the culture, managers' expectations, and technical and process expectations.

Here are four other examples of memorable moments.

The day before a person starts at his firm, the legendary sales coach Jack Daly sends chocolate or flowers to their house with a handwritten note saying, "We're so excited to have you join us tomorrow!" Jack understood how a new hire's spouse impacts how they feel about a new role. So, after the gift arrived, he knew they would both be thinking, "What a wonderful company you're starting with tomorrow, a company that really cares!"

At The Physio Co, a Melbourne-based physiotherapy provider for elderly Australians that's been awarded various places in Australia's Best Place to Work list for eleven consecutive years, new hires are provided a unique and memorable onboarding moment. To get to know each other and build trust, new hires and their manager hold a one-on-one meeting where they each go through a lifeline exercise. First, each person draws a horizontal line on a page. On the left of the line, they write the word "born," and on the right-hand side, they write "today." Then each person tells their life story, or as much as they are willing to share about the significant highs and lows. This exercise builds trust between the new hire and their manager through the vulnerability of the story and is certainly a moment that new hires remember!

For Tim Clarkson, CEO at the Sydney-based Chas Clarkson, a provider of corporate Christmas design and installation services across Australia, new hires are asked to write an introduction email to the whole company, explaining what they do and what interests them. For example, they might write, "Hi, I'm Katie, I love dogs, and I'm from Japan." Also, Tim provides a set of thank you cards with the company core values printed on them as part of their induction pack. New hires are then encouraged to assimilate into the company ritual of writing thank you cards aligned with the core values as soon as possible. The trading of handwritten thank you cards had become a cultural norm, and new hires with a pack of blank cards are encouraged to write thank you cards during their onboarding.

The fourth story comes from Mike Mirau, CEO and Founder of Tribute Printing. Mike also provides an unforgettable moment on each new hire's first day. But he does it with a fun-loving Texas style. As Mike explains it, "When people come into the office on their first day, everybody in the team is standing there and greets them. It's a big deal, with a big banner saying, 'Welcome, Brad!' We've got music playing, and it's like a sporting event. It really cements to them that they have joined a new company."

Let me be clear. Memorable moments are not providing swag. Providing a shirt or a coffee mug with the company logo is not a memorable moment. Having a clean, vacant desk and computer with login details ready for the new hire is not a memorable moment. Being prepared for a new hire to start on the first day is not memorable. That's the absolute minimum expectation. If you expect a new hire to be prepared and arrive on the agreed date, then you should also be prepared.

Part of that preparation will include inducting them into the firm. This might consist of completing the forms to get paid and pay taxes, knowing their computer login and email access, and issuing security access cards to open doors. Perhaps this is done by their manager, HR, or another admin person. Or maybe it's automated. Inductions are often a necessary part of the first day, although some firms do it prior, as part of a preboarding. Still, induction isn't a memorable moment, and it's not onboarding with their manager. That's why it's not in the onboarding sprint plan below.

Let's go back to Mike in Texas for a moment. After his exciting welcome with the banner and music, the new hire meets their manager, and together they go through a 100-day plan. First, the manager explains where they will work on their first and second weeks. Also, they explain how the new hire will need to learn all twenty-seven of their processes by the end of the onboarding period. Finally, they set the learning expectations and the manager's expectations so everyone is clear. Then through the onboarding period, at the end of every week, the manager and the new hire meet to discuss feedback and the plan for the following week.

By setting goals or milestones, Mike does something that 60% of companies don't[27]. The simple process of setting goals for a new hire can provide them with clarity, engagement, and direction. A way to think about these goals is a series of progressive learning achievements, where, for example, new hires can't complete week two until week one is complete. Or perhaps you can't complete the second month and move on to the third month until you have performed a specific action, like visiting ten clients. The onboarding sprint plan is then a series of tasks completed and discussed, transitioning the new hire through the earlier three stages – understand, learn and apply, and then embed.

While the first stage of onboarding, known as the understand stage, begins on the new hire's first day on the job, it can be valuable to prepare a new hire before they formally start work. This is known as preboarding. Preboarding is an excellent opportunity to get a new hire engaged and excited in the culture and learning process before their first day. According to one report[28] , best-in-class companies are 53% more likely than others to undertake preboarding.

Jeremy Trumble, Principal at FBT Architects in Albuquerque, New Mexico, has significantly improved his overall onboarding process using preboarding. As Jeremy explains, "We bring them in about a week before they start, so their first day isn't really their first day -- so we can talk about stuff, explain things, and answer questions without pressure. And it's really awesome for the new hire. They love it, and they get to meet their new workmates."

27 https://karesources.com/onboarding-done-right/

28 https://enboarder.com/2018/11/01/
employee-onboarding-new-hire-retention-turnover-rates/

Software developer Atlassian has a Candidate Resource Hub that candidates gain access to even before being interviewed. As they progress through to interview and job offer, they unlock different levels until their first day, where they open product crash courses and individualised 90-day action plans.

Here are a few other preboarding ideas:

- *A personalised note from their manager*

- *Electronic forms to complete payroll and admin tasks before day one*

- *A personal video from the team*

- *A virtual video tour of the office*

- *A video call with a co-worker discussing projects they will be working on*

In Table 6.2, we can see a sample onboarding sprint plan. This plan is built from the role scorecard developed earlier in this chapter. That role scorecard shows us the overall end goal, and the onboarding sprint plan explains how a new hire will reach the level of competence outlined in the role scorecard. Remember that every onboarding sprint plan is different because every candidate is different and in a different situation. They might be 80 percent similar but should be adapted for each individual. You can also download an editable version of this and other tools with a further explanation at my website, evolutionpartners.com.au.

The plan in Table 6.2 has sections divided into preboarding, day one, month one, month two, and month three. In each of those times, we're considering the cultural expectations, the manager expectations, and the technical and process expectations. It's also worth noting the areas where the new hire has achieved sufficient competency whereby they don't need to work on it any further.

One last tip: the onboarding plan must be achievable in 90 days. One

CEO I know set so many learning tasks within the onboarding sprint plan that it might have taken nine months for the new hire to complete them. Perhaps your new hire can only spend twenty hours per week on tasks you set. Ensure your goals are achievable!

The example onboarding sprint plan provided in Table 6.2 is for a sales manager who controls their time. For a worker who is not in control of their own time, like a worker paid by the hour or by the piece of work completed, the onboarding plan should be different, but the same overall principles apply.

Now, with an understanding of the role scorecard, the three stages of onboarding, and how these two help us understand and build the plan, let's look at making the onboarding sprint plan work.

	Cultural expectations	Manager's expectations	Technical and process expectations
Preboarding	Lunch with the sales team Team member photo uploaded	Visit the office for two hours to answer CEO's questions Watch Salesforce CRM intro video	Complete preboarding forms Read sales process manual Any future leave date requests
Day 1 **Onboarding meeting, Induction, Orientation**	Core values review Behaviours review Two values stories Explain daily huddles and meetings	Company history Company plans and priorities Office plan where everyone sits and their role Review personal professional development goals Verbal commitment to one another Review annual sales budget Critical success factors of the sales team	Review sales material Overview sales team performance Tour production facility with ops manager
Month 1 **Understand**	Core values stories review each week with the manager Review last year's core values award winners Understand BHAG and Brand Promise	Document personal goals and plan Review all sales material and provide a list of weaknesses and improvements needed Weekly meetings with Marketing Manager - understand lead generation and allocation process and weaknesses in the system Meet with all Sales Staff one on one and understand what makes them tick Meet 15 customers	Attend two seminars 12th and 19th June Observe three interviews for new sales staff with CEO Sit in on Sales calls with eight sales staff Attended a sales meeting with four sales staff Proficient in obtaining weekly sales reports from CRM Read Scaling Up book Read HBR article A12 in library

Month 2 **Learn & apply**	Core values stories review each week with the manager Three core values stories from the sales team Understand BHAG and Brand Promise Daily huddle with sales team embedded Cultural observations report to manager	Review personal goals and plan Implement five sales material improvements Weekly meetings with Marketing Manager - transition to new business projects One sales coaching meeting with every sales team member Meet 20 customers	Attend two seminars 7th and 21st July Participate in five interviews for new sales staff with CEO Sit in on Sales calls with 15 sales staff Attended a sales meeting with six sales staff Read Ultimate sales machine book Read HBR Article A17 in library Build a list of responses to objections with the sales team Two role-play sessions with sales team
Month 3 **Embed**	Core values stories review each week with the manager Three core values stories from outside the sales team Team building event with sales and marketing teams Five Dysfunctions of a Team cultural report	Review personal goals and plan Implement five sales material improvements Budget recommendations for every sales team member One sales coaching meeting with every sales team member Meet 20 customers Review strategy with CEO	Attend two seminars 14th and 22nd August Run five interviews for new sales staff with CEO Sit in on Sales calls with 15 sales staff Attend a sales meeting with six sales staff Weekly sales reports from CRM to leadership team Read Baseline selling book Read HBR Article A22 in library Expand list of responses to objections Two role play sessions with sales team

Table 6.2 Onboarding sprint plan example

Key Points

- *A role scorecard clarifies the role and measures each candidate against the role's expectations.*

- *A manager must build a role scorecard before advertising a vacancy or talking with candidates.*

- *The onboarding process has three distinct stages: understand, learn and apply, and then embed.*

- *Through these three stages, managers should transition from directing to coaching.*

- *Consciously creating memorable moments during onboarding can have a lasting, profound impact on people.*

- *A 90-day onboarding sprint plan should clearly outline the goals a new hire must achieve to pass their probation.*

CHAPTER 7

Making the Onboarding Sprint Plan Work

The Weekly Onboarding Meeting

Why do plans fail?

According to Harvard Business Review, 90 percent of strategies fail due to poor execution[29]. So, maybe you've built an excellent role scorecard and an onboarding sprint plan that you estimate to produce almost no onboarding debt. But that still might fail.

On November 9, 1996, when a reporter asked Mike Tyson whether he was worried about Evander Holyfield and his fight plan, he replied with the famous line, "Everyone has a plan until they get punched in the mouth." Only one out of 50 boxing writers polled at the time gave Holyfield a chance of upsetting the odds and winning the match.

As Holyfield went into that fight, the odds against him were 15-2. Yet he shocked the boxing world by winning.

He stuck to the plan and adapted it when the circumstances changed.

Seven months later, during the rematch, Holyfield's plan could never have anticipated that Tyson would bite an inch off his right ear and then bite his left. But Holyfield adapted to the situation, stuck to the plan, and won the rematch.

If you're a leader and one of your peers has implemented an onboarding sprint plan, it's disappointing to hear them say, "We dropped the weekly onboarding meeting after a month. We were just too busy, and the new hire was going pretty well." You know they planned for a new hire, but that plan won't deliver the intended success. They didn't adapt the plan to the situation. They've let the new hire down and their peers down, but most of all, they've let themselves down.

---

29 https://hbr.org/2005/10/the-office-of-strategy-management

In *Atomic Habits*, James Clear notes a question he is often asked: "'How long does it take to build a new habit?" But what people should be asking is, "How *many* does it take to form a new habit? That is, how many repetitions are required?" In Figure 7.1, you can see how James demonstrates that a behaviour can become more automatic than conscious after a certain number of repetitions by exceeding what he calls the habit line.

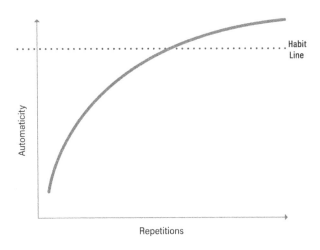

Figure 7.1 **The forming of habits from Atomic Habits**

You may recall the forgetting curve from Chapter 4, where people forget 90 percent of what they are taught a week later. When James Clear asks, "How *many* does it take to form a new habit?" through the lens of onboarding, he prompts us to ask how many repetitions it would take for a new hire to form a habit that will overcome the forgetting curve. Forming habits through a plan will only work if executed entirely and adapted as circumstances change.

The onboarding sprint plan is executed weekly with the manager and the new hire. It should lead to the successful execution of the role scorecard after the onboarding period. How you adapt the weekly meeting will depend on which onboarding stage you are in. At each weekly meeting, the manager should cover the following topics:

- *What's up, status update? Where are you stuck?*

- *Review last week's progress*

- *Review onboarding sprint plan*

- *Priorities for new hire for the next week*

A longer meeting could be held at the end of months one and two. This longer monthly meeting would also cover the following:

- *Past month's progress*

- *Onboarding sprint plan overall progress*

- *Progress toward intended performance*

- *Next month priorities*

Sometimes, a new hire's performance will differ from what you intend. It is much easier to discuss any deviation from intended performance at a weekly meeting when a manager notices it and when these discussions are easy. We can look at a three-part concept called Point Easy, as shown in Figure 7.2.

Point Easy

When a person's actual performance begins deviating from what was intended, it's much easier to talk about a slight difference between the intended performance and the actual performance. In the Point Easy diagram within Figure 7.2, you can see the intended performance over time, increasing to the right at around 45 degrees. That is the performance that is expected. Separate from that, we can see a second line, the person's actual performance, which is beginning to drift away from the first line, their intended performance. Rather than being near the intended 45 degrees, it's lower and closer to 30 degrees. Their performance is still increasing, but

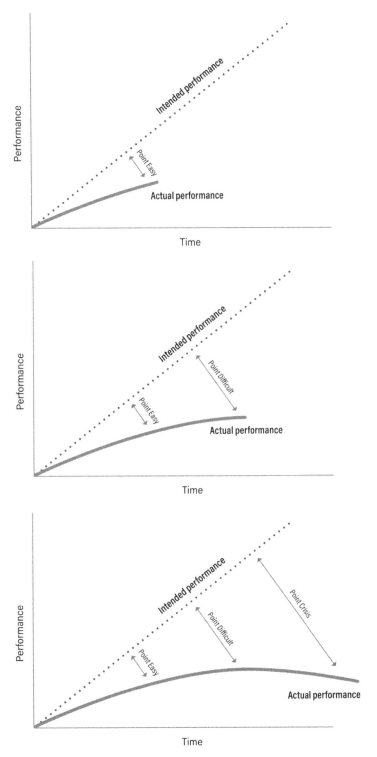

Figure 7.2 **Point Easy concept**

nowhere near the rate it should be. It's easy to have conversations at this stage and recalibrate the person back to the intended performance level.

Point Difficult

Suppose no action is taken at Point Easy, and time goes on. In that case, actual performance continues to drift away from the intended performance, and it becomes more difficult to have a conversation and recalibrate the person back to the intended performance line. In the Point Difficult diagram within Figure 7.2, actual performance is now flatlined, whereas intended performance is still increasing at around 45 degrees. At Point Difficult, people are often so far away from the intended performance that their only chance is to re-start the entire onboarding process. Recalibration back to intended performance is possible, but it isn't easy. Point Difficult is often where a manager knows that something must be done, but they are reluctant to do it or ignore it.

Point Crisis

You can't ignore point crisis. Rather than increasing at 45 degrees as intended performance prescribes, actual performance is now decreasing. When leaders are reluctant to recalibrate people at Point Difficult, their actual performance often continues to drift away from their intended performance, and leaders end up at Point Crisis. Point Crisis is stressful and expensive, leaving most leaders to wish they were back at Point Easy.

Therefore, during the weekly onboarding meeting, a manager should be looking for "Point Easy" opportunities to discuss course correction with the new hire. If left unchecked, the new hire will likely move to point crisis.

When preparing for a weekly onboarding meeting, managers should do a quick pulse check, asking themselves how the new hire is progressing in the areas of the culture, managers' expectations, and technical and process expectations. They should consider the question, "As a manager, am I suffi-ciently confident to move this person to the next stage of their onboarding?"

The answer to that question should provide a good context for discussion.

As you near the end of an onboarding period and progress into the embed stage, which involves more coaching toward the final meeting to exit a new hire's probation, the habits you have established should easily transition to your everyday management process. This includes either one-on-one reporting or reporting within a team on the progress of KPIs and priorities.

The Onboarding Buddy

A weekly onboarding meeting is effective at executing the onboarding sprint plan. However, even with the best course correction at point easy, gaps can still appear. Using a buddy to help the new hire self-correct minor issues regularly can fill those gaps.

Having a self-correcting mechanism within your onboarding process might be easier than it sounds if you utilise a buddy system. Rather than needing to course-correct every item with the new hire, a buddy system can help fill the new hire's understanding gap. And importantly, it happens from the team perspective.

At San Francisco-based Salesforce, a buddy system helps fill gaps in understanding for new hires. As Rolan Myer, who has onboarded three buddies since he started working there, explains, "There is no amount of documentation that can achieve as much as someone walking and talking you through some of the basics about working here."[30]

Typically, an onboarding buddy helps new hires:

- *Learn how to navigate the office structure and complete administrative tasks*

---

30 https://medium.com/@salesforce/
how-we-use-onboarding-buddies-at-salesforce-and-why-you-should-too-49d825fa9771

- *Meet other team members and establish an extended network between cross-functional departments*

- *Understand the culture from a non-managers perspective*

- *Develop friendships that last beyond the initial onboarding period*

From the cultural onboarding perspective, those last two points make a significant difference when considering a new hire. As Andy Kang, also from Salesforce, points out, "I don't know how long it would have taken me to be able to run an assignment without an onboarding buddy. My onboarding buddy was incredibly helpful as my go-to guy for all questions and confusions, whether they were technical or more about the workplace and team."

In my research, respondents who had only one person involved in the onboarding process, and no buddy, were four times more likely to disagree that their onboarding process positively contributes to their culture. And in other research by HCI, 87 percent of organisations[31] with a buddy program agree that it's an effective way to speed up a new hire's proficiency. Indeed, another type of buddy program, the apprenticeship system, has worked effectively for hundreds of years to help new hires become proficient.

So how should you select a new hire's buddy?

I've seen senior people suggest that new hires take current processes or cultural initiatives with a grain of salt. This cultural influence can be confusing or conflicting for the new hire. Also, there's a common misconception that only senior people can teach. One of the best ways to learn is to teach others what you have learned. And so, it can be best to select your new hire's buddy from some of the most recent employees who have completed their onboarding.

Buddies should be selected from recent hires because:

---

31 https://www.g2.com/articles/onboarding-statistics

- *They still remember the process.*

- *They have more empathy for the new hire and what they are experiencing.*

- *Having to teach someone else reinforces their learnings.*

It reinforces process compliance because more established team members who aren't adhering to the process aren't passing on their bad habits.

When preparing recent hires to become buddies for a new hire, you can also ask them to list a few things they didn't learn when they were new hires. This question helps the buddy prepare a better experience and creates a self-improvement loop to pick up any items that managers might miss in inductions or onboarding sprint plans.

Looking for feedback to improve the onboarding sprint plan is one of the questions that Sandra Francis, People and Culture Manager at Aventus, a large format retail centre owner and operator across Australia, asks new hires. Sandra regularly checks in with new hires to ask questions, including the following:

- *Have you been welcomed?*

- *Do you know what's expected of you in the role?*

- *Do you feel you can be productive in your role?*

- *Are you having regular one-on-one meetings with your manager?*

- *Has your onboarding sprint plan helped your onboarding, and what suggestions do you have?*

Sandra isn't the new hire's manager or buddy, but she looks for gaps and ensures that things are running smoothly.

A buddy provides a connection between the new hire and the team in a way a manager can't. The manager is a part of the team, but not the same way a new hire's peers are, and a buddy can fill the gaps left by other parts of the onboarding process.

Formally Concluding an Onboarding

Through this research project, as I spent countless hours looking over the data, there have been many surprises for me, with some things that I felt might have been more important at first and other things I took for granted that mattered. One of the things that I found most surprising was the importance of a meeting to formally complete a new hire's onboarding.

Let's look at three key correlations in Figure 7.3 between respondents who didn't have a formal documented meeting to end an onboarding and other outcomes.

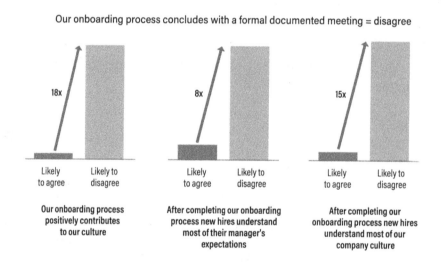

Figure 7.3 **Correlation to other questions for respondents without a final meeting**

Respondents who didn't have a formal documented meeting to conclude an onboarding were:

- *Eighteen times more likely to disagree that their onboarding process positively contributes to their culture*

- *Eight times more likely to disagree that after completing their onboarding process, new hires understand most of their managers' expectations*

- *Fifteen times more likely to disagree that after completing their onboarding process, new hires understand most of their company culture*

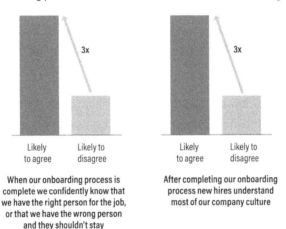

Our onboarding process concludes with a formal documented meeting = agree

3x	3x
Likely to agree — Likely to disagree	Likely to agree — Likely to disagree

When our onboarding process is complete we confidently know that we have the right person for the job, or that we have the wrong person and they shouldn't stay

After completing our onboarding process new hires understand most of our company culture

Figure 7.4 **Correlation to other questions for respondents who held a final meeting**

Next, we will look at two key correlations in Figure 7.4 from the opposite angle, between respondents who did have a formal documented meeting to end an onboarding.

Respondents who held a formal documented meeting to conclude an onboarding were:

- *Three times more likely to agree that when their onboarding process is complete, they confidently know that they have the right person for the job, or that they have the wrong person who shouldn't stay*

- *Three times more likely to agree that after completing their onboarding, new hires understand most of their company culture*

Often, managers can miss a formal documented meeting to conclude an onboarding period, or perhaps it only becomes a part of the process when a person isn't performing as expected. Yet this simple formality not only connects to key outcomes, as demonstrated in Figures 7.3 and 7.4; it also provides several other benefits.

- *It provides a final date when new hires must have completed tasks and goals.*

- *As noted in Chapter 1, it provides the last opportunity to exit a new hire without legal ramifications in many countries.*

- *Managers can provide new hires formal written feedback summarising the whole onboarding period.*

- *It establishes a formal performance management feedback environment for the future.*

- *It provides an opportunity to recognise achievements and create memorable moments.*

- *It enables the manager to transition to standard operating and formally set and commence the following quarters' KPIs and priorities for the new hire.*

In preparing for the last onboarding meeting, you can use two simple tools. First, consider the three questions from Chapter 2 about onboarding debt:

1 *Are they capable of succeeding in the role?*

2 *Do they understand what it takes to succeed in the role?*

3 *Do they want to succeed in the role?*

You can rate the new hire a score out of ten on each of these questions, which should be easy by now if you've been running weekly meetings. Once you have a rating, you can answer the final question listed below, as discussed earlier in this chapter. "As a manager, am I sufficiently confident to complete this person's onboarding and release them from their probation period?"

Once you've answered that question and are prepared for the meeting, a great way to begin a final onboarding meeting is by completing the sentence "We hired you because." Your explanation should include aspects of the culture and performance of the new hire. Then, the manager can recount specific stories that connect with the company's core values and tasks the new hire has completed in a particular manner.

If the new hire has successfully completed their onboarding, this final meeting can also be considered the first performance review. This means discussing the positive and negative aspects of the new hire's performance. In the 2014 HBR article, "Your employees want the negative feedback you hate to give," Jack Zenger and Joseph Folkman detailed their research that people are three times more likely to prefer receiving negative feedback than avoid giving negative feedback. Of course, this is in the context of the negative feedback being constructive. So, when formally concluding an onboarding, the manager must include straightforward, demonstrable ways the new hire can improve along with praise and commentary. This approach establishes the habit and constructive mechanism for future coaching and improvement. The new hire should also know the date of the next performance review, and the sooner, the better.

Managers should not discuss salary at the final onboarding meeting or performance reviews. Salary reviews should be separate meetings with separate agendas in a different process. As one team I work with explained, "We pay team members well in line with the industry, inflation, and the role. We keep individual performance separate, and we expect performance around the role scorecard."

Having answered the question "This is why we hired you" and reviewed the new hire's performance through the onboarding sprint plan, providing feedback about their performance, you can then turn to the future with the new hire. You can consider the original role scorecard and how the new hire meets its criteria. Also, perhaps it is time to start the new hire working on broader company priorities and projects beyond their original job role. Whatever it is, it's essential to establish these goals for the coming quarter with the new hire providing clarity on their direction.

Finally, the last meeting provides an excellent opportunity to recognise a memorable moment. Perhaps you could throw a small celebration with the team or give the person a mention in the corporate newsletter. Maybe you could take the new hire out for lunch. The opportunity presents itself to make that moment a ritual for all new hires and become part of the company story.

Formally concluding an onboarding process can be a simple, formal meeting that produces tangible benefits before, during, and after for both the new hire and the new hire's manager.

Key Points

- *Managers should review and progress the onboarding sprint plan at the weekly meeting.*

- *When new hires complete their onboarding, they should transition to an ongoing set of KPIs and priorities.*

- *An onboarding buddy can fill the gaps left by other parts of the onboarding process.*

- *A meeting to conclude a new hire's onboarding provides a formal conclusion and feedback and establishes a constructive relationship for new hires and managers to move forward.*

Next Steps

Thank you for reading *Onboarded*.

My primary objective in writing this book was to address what I view as the most significant opportunity in leadership today, which carries an enormous cost. I then wanted to take that opportunity and provide you with a simple, practical, and actionable tool that you can immediately implement into your firm that will produce a significant impact.

As I noted in Chapter 5, for most readers, the most significant hurdle they will face in implementing this process is that onboarding has no clear ownership, no clear outcome, and is a part-time process. These are not insignificant challenges. As a business community, we haven't reached the point where it is so rare to find effective onboarding without good reason, even though it is so very expensive if done poorly.

And as I've demonstrated through the first five chapters of this book, the cost of not applying a simple process, as I've shown in a disciplined manner owned by the direct manager of a new hire, can be outrageous.

To give you the best chance to successfully implement the concepts in this book, consider these five best practices.

Begin at the Beginning

Your first job should be to identify the first new hire with whom to use this process. Ideally, it will be the next role you plan to hire. You may be tempted to immediately build role scorecards for all positions within your firm, but I've found you can have a much greater chance of success by starting with a single vacant role. Select your next role, build a role scorecard, and then develop an onboarding sprint plan.

Perhaps you might not run this process for the first time, and instead, it would be a department manager or another leader. If that's the case, I encourage the new hire's manager to read this book, and then you or someone else can coach them through the process. I also have another book

Onboarded for Managers which is a short easy to read guide that you can provide to your team members to understand how and why to implement the principles and tools in this book.

When you have run a new hire through the onboarding process for the first time, if they are successful in the end, it's a good idea to ask them, *"Can you name three things you wish you learned when you onboarded?"* Then you will identify holes in your process from the new hire's perspective that you can improve each time you run the process. You can also ask the new hire's manager who is running the onboarding process, *"Can you name three ideas to improve our onboarding process?"* This continual feedback loop is essential because you won't get it right the first time, and there is no substitute for feedback from users. As I like to say to leadership teams, this book is an example of best practice. Your job now is to figure out how to make best practice work best in your organisation.

Use Agendas

The risk with any new initiative is that things will revert to how they were. It's the risk that the new tool won't stick. New initiatives need two points of accountability. First, a person who is accountable to report is required, and second, a time when the accountable person will report. I encourage you to build an onboarding status update into weekly meeting agendas. If any manager or leader is onboarding a new hire, they should provide a quick status update at a meeting with their manager. For example, it could be as simple as the statement, "Kate is ahead of schedule on her onboarding sprint plan, and we are 75 percent complete. At this rate, she is likely to pass her onboarding at the end." It doesn't need to be a thirty-minute conversation, just a status update. An update should tell the meeting delegates that I'm sticking to our process and that the candidate is likely to be a successful or unsuccessful fit at my current assessment. The example shown above would take less than ten seconds.

But, if the onboarding sprint plan isn't being followed, or the new hire isn't likely to succeed, then this short, weekly check-in should provide a simple way to identify any issues and address them sooner rather than later.

Use Data

To write this book, I've researched a lot of data from my own survey and interviews, and many leading publications. Suppose you're going to the trouble of implementing an onboarding process as I've advocated. In that case, I suggest you consider measuring and monitoring some of the metrics I've highlighted in this book. For example, what was your attrition or retention rate last year? How much did that cost? As I've outlined in this book, how do managers rate recent hires' understanding?

Also, you can survey new hires about the process to see if and how it is helping them.

If you understand and regularly measure some of these items, you can gain the confidence that it is making a difference.

Use a Coach

Top athletes and sports teams know it's impossible to achieve peak performance without a coach. The right coach for you, for your leadership team, with the right fit and an external perspective, will genuinely challenge you to go beyond your comfort zone.

There is no doubt that some coaches are better than others in the business world and the sports world. For example, you wouldn't expect a youth soccer coach to be a great coach in the national league with a team of elite athletes.

Like in the sports world, the elite coaches are in great demand and will cost more but can significantly impact a serious business endeavouring to thrive. You need to be confident that any coach is the right fit for you.

If you need help implementing these tools, my firm Evolution Partners will be able to help you, or we can introduce you to some of our certified coaching partners across the globe. You can find me at brad.giles@evolutionpartners.com.au, where I'd love to hear from you.

Enjoy the journey

Every time a new person joins a team, the team fundamentally reinvents itself. The purpose of this book is that every time you reinvent your team, it helps you make that new team a better team.

Because better teams produce better results, it's more enjoyable to be part of a better team.

Even though there is a lot of work to do in this book, work that takes time, the intent is to ultimately give you more time.

The more you grow as a leader, the more you recognise that a leader's job is to grow the people around you. To grow the people who report to you. Then, when those people are the right people, doing the right things the right way, because they understand the processes, culture, and expectations, your entire team is more effective and efficient, and your job more enjoyable. And it also makes the journey more enjoyable for everyone.

So, smile, laugh, celebrate the wins, and enjoy the journey with your team.